WATCHING OVER THE HEART

WATCHING OVER THE HEART

*Is there hope
for deep, spiritual transformation?*

Michael C. Sharrett

Metokos Press
Narrows, VA 24124

Published by Metokos Press, Inc., committed to providing materials easily accessible to the average reader while at the same time presenting biblical truth from within the framework of biblical and confessional churches of Reformed and Presbyterian heritage. Visit us on the web at www.metokospress.com.

Cover design by Chip Evans, Walker-Atlanta, Atlanta, GA.

Printed in the United States by Lightning Source, LaVergne, TN.

ISBN 978-0-9742331-3-0

Dedicated to Dowell,
whose encouragement, example and friendship
inspired me to press on,

and to Janice,
whose love and faithfulness
have been a blessing beyond measure.

Foreword

"Suppose," asked D. L. Moody, "that a man would advertise to take photographs of the heart; would he get many customers?"

Good question, easily answered: because the heart is *"deceitful and desperately wicked,"* no one in his right mind would want this cesspool at the core of his being exposed for all the world to see. But the Bible does expose it. And Mike Sharrett does faithfully, with tough love, expound and explain what the Bible says about it. However, Mike's primary focus is really not the heart, it is God. Though he carefully and pastorally examines what Scripture says about why we do not whole-heartedly love God, he at the same time exalts the magnificence, majesty and mercy of the One who changes cesspools into clear springs and transforms self-love into Triune-God-love.

Clearly, compassionately, cheerfully, Mike describes how God makes this miraculous heart-change happen. He calls us to *"taste and see that the Lord is good,"* to make Him *"the one thing that we seek after,"* *"...to know the love of Christ that surpasses knowledge, that we may be filled with all the fullness of God..."* (Ephesians 3:19).

The glory of it all is this, that though "the hideous sight, the naked human heart" is seen by God alone, He sees the hearts of His own as beautiful, cleansed by Christ's blood. Our filthiness cannot be photographed, because it is covered by the righteousness of the Son of God, our Savior. So, believer in Jesus, rejoice, and live freely before your wonderful God!

Paul G. Settle
Dallas, TX

Acknowledgements

I am very grateful to Christ Jesus my Lord and Savior for the variety of influences with which He has graced my life: spiritual mentors Skip Ryan, Ed Clowney, Tim Keller, and Sam Logan; the faculty of Westminster Theological Seminary, Philadelphia, 1985-88; the encouragement of my friends Tom Darnell, Randy Draughon, Ron Gray, John Kuebler, John Tinnin, and Brian Webster; the friendship of Caleb LaRue, Rick Parsons, John Dantzler, Fred Archer, Jim Jackson and David Flowers; my mother, Emily, and father, Allan, and brothers Al and Dave; my friend Dowell Stackpole, without whose encouragement I doubt this book would have been written; the many precious saints at Ft. Worth PCA and Redeemer PCA in Lynchburg, VA; my children Mike, Luke and Laura; my in-laws Ted and Doris Beechwood; and my wife Janice, whose love and faithfulness have been a blessing beyond measure.

Contents

Part 4: The Heart at Work

Introduction

"Am I as impressed with God as it seems I should be?"

For the past twenty-five years, I have had the privilege, both as a career counselor and as a pastor, to write many recommendations for individuals setting their sails for the academy or the marketplace. Each reference requires essentially the same assessment: based on my familiarity with the applicant, give my honest impression of his character and abilities. Thankfully, I can't remember ever having to report, "I'm not very impressed."

What if you or I were asked to write a recommendation for God? What would we say are our honest impressions of His character and abilities? Yes, I know … what an odd question! Whoever thought they needed to write a recommendation for God? If anyone in the universe does *not* need a reference, certainly it is the Lord Almighty. He who answers to no one is the standard against which all moral glory is measured. But, for everyone who *says* they believe in God, the fact is, their lifestyle, commitments and daily choices inevitably reveal what they truly believe about God's character (His heart) and abilities (what He is able to do). Personally, I must admit that is an arresting thought! Could it *really* be true that, if I believe in God, the *way* I live (what I pursue, how I speak and act, everything I choose to do or not to do), and the *reason* I live (my motives and inner drives, what I delight in or find ultimately satisfying), constitute, de facto, my truest impressions of God?

The longer I'm in pastoral ministry, the more I continue to be intrigued by this question: why do so many of us who believe in God seem too often—dare we say it—to be "not very impressed" with Him? Why does God function in our lives less like a very present, loving Father and more like the sun? I don't doubt it's there; it just seems 93 million miles away and way too intense to look at directly.

Consider it another way: although you and I go to church, can recite the Apostles' Creed, and celebrate Easter and Christmas, who would conclude from observing our true passions that we were indelibly impressed with the wonder, glory, majesty, splendor and beauty of God? Who would say, "This person's life marches in step with Someone much bigger than himself?" Would those who know us well believe it if we confessed with the psalmist: *"Whom have I in heaven but you; and besides you, I desire nothing on earth?"* (Ps. 73:25) He desires *nothing* but God! What can that mean? Don't we all share many good, God-given desires? Whatever he means, clearly the psalmist is deeply impressed with God. Can I *honestly* say that? Intellectually, I think I *should*, but why do I find it difficult experientially?

Are you deeply impressed with God?

Here's the simplest way to address my concern: are *you* deeply impressed with God? What would it look like if God *had* made a deep impression on your heart? If your heart was warm wax and God impressed the seal of His beauty on it, how different would you be? When I was eighteen, the importance of physical health was deeply impressed upon my heart. My dad suffered several heart attacks at the same time all the dietary studies on fats, cholesterol and heart disease made the headlines. Deeply affected, and driven by self-preservation, I made changes in my diet and exercise commitments, which remain vital to me to this day. The same is true with your spiritual heart. When God impresses Himself upon you, lasting and vital changes follow. This book intends to explore those changes.

If the Bible is accurate, those who know God personally invariably find their hearts profoundly impressed with His character and abilities. They can't remain the person they were before they knew Him. He definitely makes a good and lasting impression upon them, silly as it sounds to say! But surely we understand that dynamic; isn't it similar to the way you feel in the presence of an exceedingly powerful or important person? Aren't you instinctively compelled to please, admire or draw close to them? Don't you want to tell your friends all about the incident where you met a cultural,

2

political or athletic superstar? Well, how much *more* could it be true of God, a person of impeccable character and unlimited abilities?

No one who reckons honestly with God comes away with an evaluation of *unimpressive*. Please notice that I asserted, "reckons *honestly* with God." Not everyone who reckons with God feels impressed; the Bible is unapologetically transparent about this fact! Jesus, God in the flesh, met with decidedly mixed reviews in His earthly ministry. Immediately following His first sermon in His hometown Nazareth, *"all in the synagogue were filled with rage and rose up"* to run Him off a cliff; yet, in a village of the despised Samaritans the whole town begged him to stay (compare Luke 4:29 with John 4:40). Some counted Jesus their dearest friend, while others tried to stone Him as a most hated enemy. Some stood at a distance in skeptical curiosity, while others hung on His every word (some literally clung to His body!). At the start, the multitudes flocked to hear Jesus, yet by the end of His ministry, even His closest friends deserted Him.

Perhaps most similar to many of us, some people were superficially impressed—they experienced a fleeting *awe* as they witnessed His deeds and heard His teachings—but, at the end of the day, they went on to more pressing, personal matters. They paid their respects when appropriate, perhaps were sentimentally touched; but all the while maintained basic rights to their own schedules, reputations and preferences. How is it that they (I'm certain I also) could be *unimpressed* with the presence and claims of the King of Kings?

To be sure, all who recognized Jesus' identity experienced the profound impression of His glory. They became, in Paul's words, a *"new creation"* (2 Cor. 5:17), supernaturally changed by His presence. Apparently they saw what the Apostle John testified concerning Jesus: *"The word* [Jesus] *was God and the word became flesh and dwelt among us...and we beheld His glory, glory as of the only begotten of the Father, full of grace and truth."* (John 1:1-17) They loved Him and gave up all to follow Him boldly without reservation. What a recommendation: this man deserves *all* of me! What did these followers possess that the others lacked? To what were so many other folks blind that His faithful followers were blessed to see?

3

What kind of response does God want from you?

Perhaps we discover the answer to that question by pressing another one: what kind of response *does* God want from you? Is He content for you merely to believe that He exists while allowing you essentially to self-style your life? Is it enough, *from God's perspective*, that you claim to believe in Him, give Him an hour on Sunday, say a prayer when you need extra help, but, for the most part, keep your heart exclusively to yourself? Will God merely be one of among many entries on your list of people you know? For a long time I lived like that. We might call this "liaise faire Christianity." God does His thing in heaven while I do my thing on earth, and when I've finished my course, He just beams me up! Sure, whenever necessary, I ask for a push if the going gets tough, but I control the steering wheel. Do you see that this form of religion never comes to grips with how much of *you* God wants? It is actually driven by how much of *God* you care to desire. For the longest time I really had no idea how much of me God wanted!

So, have you thought about that? What does God want from you? At one level, it isn't difficult to imagine that God desires from you the same things you expect from others: respect, honor of your personhood, a fair hearing, honest appraisal of your work, unbiased evaluation of your character, impartial assessment of your abilities and submission to your authority (if it happens to be due you). God is a person in some ways like us, so we must resist the temptation to depersonalize Him. He has a name; He is not an impersonal force. He has a distinct, unchanging character and personality, a way of accomplishing purposes, and specific things He loves and hates. He has feelings and a will, as well as an intense interest in the affairs of this world, which He tells us He made for His own pleasure and upholds for His own glory. As a parent, our heavenly Father has compassion on His children and longs for their welfare. As the friend of sinners, our older brother Jesus sticks close and never desserts us to our foes. As our advocate, the Holy Spirit counsels, comforts and convicts.

At another level (and this does not always strike us intuitively), because God is the Almighty—the sovereign Creator and Sustainer of the universe, whose wisdom is unsearchable, whose knowledge is infinite, whose presence fills every square inch of the universe, whose power is unlimited, who is self-existent and completely independent of His creation—why *wouldn't* He be due your reverence and adoration above everything else?

We understand this in life; we instinctively praise that which is excellent. All the crowds at PGA events follow Tiger Woods; all the fans jammed into the arenas when Michael Jordan suited up. Since God has no rivals, can you think of *any* good reason why He *alone* ought not to be worshiped and glorified by you and me? Psalm 29:9 says, *"Everything in His temple says, 'glory'!"* Revelation depicts those in His presence in heaven, who see God for who He truly is, constantly declare, *"You are worthy!"* (Revelation 4:11) They cannot resist declaring what they see: God's utter worth! We on earth are called to do nothing less.

The Bible, in a variety of ways, describes what should be humanity's logical, sensible, reasonable response to God. It depicts *"the fear of the Lord"* (Proverbs 1:7); declares, *"Let all the inhabitants of the world stand in awe of Him"* (Psalm 33:8); directs, *"Let all the earth be silent before Him"* (Habakkuk 2:20); and urges, *"Delight yourself in the Lord"* (Psalm 37:4). The Apostle Paul wrote one of the most dramatic exclamations of the surpassing worth of God. *"Oh, the depth of the riches and wisdom and knowledge of God! How unsearchable are His judgments and how inscrutable His ways! 'For who has known the mind of the Lord, or who has been His counselor? Or who has given a gift to Him that He might be repaid?' For from Him and through Him and to Him are all things. To Him be glory forever. Amen."* (Romans 11:33-36) Honestly, I read those words and wonder, "Am I really there?" Am I as impressed with God as it *seems* I should be?

The simplest way to sum up what God wants from you, therefore, is that you allow Him to have His way with your heart—to make His fullest impression on it. The surest evidence that you agree is your honest, sincere, *joyful* acknowledgment of the worth that is due Him. The Bible calls that *praise*; literally hundreds of times the Bible invokes us to praise God! If we look carefully at the Bible we notice that the worship we owe Him is a certain kind of adoration. I've praised many things in my life, but not always with joy. The accomplishments of technology, science, medicine, artists and athletes, for example, evoke awe and high compliments, but they are not necessarily laced with joy. God says to you, *"sing for* joy *to the Lord...shout to Him with* joy...*serve Him with* gladness..." (Psalm 100) True praise springs from a heart that is *joyfully* impressed with the surpassing worth of God in comparison to everything else, including oneself! Therefore, true praise flows out of a humble heart. Psalm 34:1-2 captures this. *"... I will* bless *the Lord at all times, His* praise *shall continually be in my mouth...let us* exalt *His name together... the* humble *will hear it and rejoice."*

So if God is exactly who He claims to be, it follows that you *must* treasure and seek Him with all your heart, soul, strength and mind. Jesus said this is the *"great and foremost commandment"* (Matt. 22:38). Or, put it in these terms: my impression of God actually corresponds directly to His impression on me. If that's true, then why *don't* we esteem God highly and consistently? Why aren't we more impressed with God, more caught up in His beauty? Why are we so easily enamored with all the good things He gives, rather than with the Giver of all good things? These questions cause a rattling in my conscience.

Grappling with some tough questions

Eventually, an honest truth-seeker will grapple with these concerns. I eventually had to admit that if I *am* disinterested in these questions, minimize them or just skirt this serious problem—*being unimpressed with God*—it actually proves the point. The evidence that I *am* unimpressed *is* my sustained reluctance to admit it, or to do anything about it. Many of us hear about people who pursue God with wholehearted abandon, or with single-minded, undistracted devotion, and we do one of two things. Either we put them in a special category of those untouchables "I'll *never* be like" (such as Mother Teresa, Billy Graham or a self-sacrificing missionary), or we feel threatened. Such commitment exposes something in us that's discomforting. It exposes the proclivity in us to pursue God on our own terms. We tend to respect the person who excels sacrificially to win an Olympic medal or to build a successful business, but we're quick to brand as *fanatic* one who pursues God unreservedly. But is that *really* so undesirable? Why do we feel the need to distance ourselves from a passionate pursuit of God?

I remember one of the ways this vividly came home to my heart. I pray every night with each of my children. One time I was praying for my oldest son, then in the fifth grade, who showed some decent potential in sports (which did not disappoint me, being a washed-up old athlete!) I began to pray, "Lord, help him fulfill his greatest potential in all things." But, what I meant was, "Help him to excel in sports!" Admittedly, that is certainly not a bad thing in itself. However, I realized that I wanted him to excel in sports *more* than I wanted him to excel in his Christian faith (unquestionably a much better thing!) It was one of those instances when you feel like God has shown you that your priorities are significantly skewed. More impressive on my heart was the prospect (however farfetched!) of athletic fame and big-league contracts, than the most precious thing in the world, the impact of God in his heart. I forced myself to reason it out. Would I *really* rather see him excel in sports with relatively brief consequences, or see him be deeply impressed by God with eternal consequences? Would I rather he be a millionaire baseball star for a *fourth* of his life, or possess the spiritual collateral to deal with his marriage, professional disappointments, children's challenges, cancer—you name it—for *all* of his life? (Of course, I'm not saying you can't do both; the issue is, what captures the *first* and *greatest* concern of your life.)

As if that wasn't convicting enough, God exposed me again once I changed how I prayed for my son. I did begin to pray, "Lord, help him be all that he is created to be as a Christian." That was good! But that prayer for him, like a boomerang, came soaring back into my own heart. Would I pray the same for *myself?* My reluctance to take God seriously began to be increasingly exposed as I gradually wrestled honestly with questions like these.

How often do you think of God? How often do you sense the pleasure of His character? To whom have you ever boasted about the greatness of God? How often do you render heartfelt thanks to God for *everything* you have? How often do you take *delight* in what He has made? How quick are you to acknowledge His sovereign control over all your affairs? How often do you wonder, "What would please Him right now?" How long have you simply meditated on God in one sitting? How much of your paycheck does He deserve? What are you doing to allow God to make His impression regularly on your heart?

These types of questions begin to gnaw at the heart when you ponder claims of biblical writers such as this. *"One thing I have asked of the Lord, that I will seek after; that I may dwell in the house of the Lord all the days of my life, to gaze upon the beauty of the Lord and to inquire in His temple."* (Ps. 27:4) So impressed with God is King David that he ultimately desires *one thing*: to be in the presence of the Lord, to look upon the beauty of the Lord. This is a man who had it all—kingly authority, military power, riches, every kind of pleasure, poetic gifts, popularity, intellect, charisma, wisdom—yet they all paled in comparison to *one thing*: the presence of God.

This book attempts to uncover the biblical explanation for our *apparent* disinterest in the beauty of the Lord, who is undeniably the most glorious, weighty person in the universe. Don't we know that, at least to *some* degree? Deep in our conscience, we know it *has* to be true, but if we truly believed it, I maintain that we would be impressed much more consistently with His character and abilities. The tragic fact, for me anyway, is I remain much more impressed with many other things. My goal in this book, therefore, is straightforward: to help you take your place with the psalmist who knows, *"God is my exceeding joy"* (Ps. 43:4); the sage who reflects, *"Nothing I desire compares with you."* (Prov. 3:15); the Apostle who says, *"To live is Christ, to die is gain"* (Phil. 1:21); the king who claims, *"Your love is better than life"* (Ps. 63:3); and the singer who confesses, *"My soul longs for you."* (Ps. 42:1) Said another way, the invitation of this book is captured by the psalmist's words, *"Let all who seek Thee rejoice and be glad in Thee; Let those who love Thy salvation say continually, 'The Lord be magnified!' "* (Ps. 40:16)

Yes, that is the place I need to be. I know because God's word says so! That poet found the place where a glad heart is deeply impressed with the splendor of God. From that place, you will want to say to God, "Be magnified! Show me more! Make Yourself bigger! Put Your character on the Jumbotron big screen of my heart. One small glance at a Rembrandt masterpiece isn't enough! Two brief lines from Handel's *Messiah* won't nearly suffice! Just a sip of fine wine or morsel of superb food won't satisfy! A mere nanosecond of romance leaves one empty! Give me more!" So David invites us to *"taste and see that the Lord is good"* (Ps. 34:8), and Paul prays, *"open the eyes of my heart..."* (Eph. 1:18).

It took me too long to start caring!

I want to confess how long it has taken me to actually *care* that I am deeply impressed with God (and I've attended church virtually my whole life). Perhaps two examples will help illustrate the genesis of spiritual change. A university student who attended my church shared with me some of the stages in her spiritual pilgrimage. She explained the point at which God began to impress her heart deeply. What was the precipitating event? Although she was raised in a Christian home, she always attended church and helped lead the youth group, she woke up one morning at college thinking, "I don't need God. I'm living as if God makes no difference in my life." She knew that perspective contradicted her core beliefs and began to seek His grace and presence in a deeper way. Why, after all, go to church if not to meet with God in a deeply impressive way?

This student's experience illustrates a truism. It is usually the case that those who are well off, well educated, well gifted, well physically, and well adjusted, have a difficult time sensing their deep need of God. Jesus said the kingdom of God is closer to the poor because they don't have the external props to deceive them about their spiritual poverty. The journey to spiritual health starts with a sense of spiritual bankruptcy. We aim to examine the discovery of that bankruptcy in the following chapters.

Personally, I remember, in a most formative season of spiritual transformation, a conversation with a colleague on the University of Virginia faculty. I conveyed enthusiastically the joy of experiencing the grace of Christ. (I suppose you'd say God was making a fresh impression on my heart.) I don't recall what I said or for how long I rambled. But I will never forget this colleague's response. "Mike, you're taking this all *much* too seriously." Intuitively, I knew that was wrong. How could I take God *too* seriously? Is the alternative to be *unimpressed* with God? Or is there some middle ground where *we* control or regulate the extent God is permitted to impress our hearts? I was enabled by grace to think it through. No, the tragedy lies with those who refuse to take God seriously enough.

By God's sheer kindness, I have come to believe that if any of us is unimpressed with God, the problem isn't with Him! God hides from no one. Since He is zealous for all His creation to behold His glory, there must be something wrong with us. So we must have spiritual integrity: the reason we're not deeply impressed with God is simply that it is not in our hearts to be so! Those willing to explore the problem and to embrace God's solution are promised this reward by God Himself: *"...to know the love of Christ that surpasses knowledge, that you may be filled with all the fullness of God..."* (Eph. 3:19). (Do you sense that this verse promises too much?) I want to be there, and I want you there, too!

The Apostle Peter wrote to folks like you and me, who never laid eyes on Jesus, yet, by the transforming grace of God's Spirit, became deeply impressed with God. *"Though you have not seen Him, you love Him. Though you do not now see Him, you believe in Him and rejoice with joy that is inexpressible and filled with glory, obtaining the outcome of your faith, the salvation of your souls."* (1 Peter 1:8-9)

If you desire *inexpressible joy*, I humbly invite you to explore with me how God makes His impression upon our hearts. If you can't honestly say you're interested in a pursuit of such joy, perhaps you'll read on to discover a biblical explanation for why. The basic thesis of this book is that we change spiritually, albeit gradually, as God impresses the glory of Christ upon our hearts. We grow, therefore, *"in the grace and knowledge of the Lord Jesus Christ."* (2 Peter 3:18) The knowledge of Jesus Christ involves *both* the Spirit impressing upon our hearts His glory revealed in the Scriptures, *and* the discovery of the depth of our own sin, forsaking it for Him who is infinitely more delightful. We turn first to the nature of the heart.

PART I

THE HEART UNDERSTOOD

¹My son, do not forget my teaching, but let your heart keep my commandments; ²For length of days and years of life, and peace they will add to you; ³Do not let kindness and truth leave you; bind them around your neck, write them on the tablet of your heart. ⁴So you will find favor and good repute in the sight of God and man. ⁵Trust in the Lord with all your heart, and do not lean on your own understanding. ⁶In all your ways acknowledge Him, and He will make your paths straight. ⁷Do not be wise in your own eyes; fear the Lord and turn away from evil.

Proverbs 3:1-7

Know Your Heart

"What you don't know about yourself can hurt you."

It felt slightly rude interrupting, but he knew I had no malicious intentions. In casual conversation, a close associate kept using the phrase "me and him." Upon my correction, we agreed that proper English required us to reverse the order to "him and me." Then I couldn't help editorializing, "Ah, but isn't it our *nature* to put ourselves first? That's why we tend to speak that way—we're all so naturally self-centered!" My associate responded with frank innocence, "I didn't know that!"

I confess to being somewhat surprised. He honestly didn't know his *nature* was to put himself first, despite the fact that he had gone to church all his life! The truth is, we all are profoundly self-centered, though some of us see it in ourselves more clearly than others do. If you listen to the way people talk, what they choose to complain about and where their focus seems to be, some people wear their self-centeredness with more sparkle than others do! What's my point? If you don't know your nature is to be self-centered, then you don't know yourself. What you don't know about yourself could really harm you. That's why the doctor says you should get a regular check-up. That's why we now see billboards advertising the full-body scan for complete peace of mind.

The Bible tells us it is extremely important to know what we are naturally like spiritually—to have a full scan of the inner person, or what the Bible calls *the heart*. The reasoning isn't so much according to the Greek philosophical notions "know thyself" or "the unexamined life is not worth living." The Bible's concern is that we know ourselves honestly, so that we can know God truly!

The Bible offers something much greater than mere self-awareness or self-actualization; it holds forth the promise of friendship with God. Knowing God intimately is fundamentally a matter of the heart; this is where God makes His impression upon us. Apparently, it is far too easy to relate to God in formal, empty ritual. Jesus lamented the Judaism of His day. *"These people honor me with their lips, but their* hearts *are far from me."* (Is. 29:13, Matt. 15:8, Mark 7:6) It is critical to understand that we relate not just to God out of the heart, but also to all of life out of the heart. It is in the heart that we take instructions for how we choose to act. It is as if we write a script on the heart for what we want in life. The book of Proverbs acknowledges this, and therefore exhorts us to *"bind kindness and truth around your neck, write them on the tablet of your* heart.*"* (Prov. 3:3)

Have you ever considered such an idea: *writing on your heart?* Many people write well on tablets of paper (or computer screens). But who learns to write well on the tablet of his heart? The wise man does, says Proverbs, for life and death hang in the balance. Allow me to introduce you to the book of Proverbs. Proverbs, as a biblical genre, is wisdom literature. The overarching concern of this book is *the fear of the Lord* (not *fear* as in being afraid or servile, but *fear* as revering, honoring, adoring God as LORD). *"The fear of the Lord is the beginning of knowledge…"* (Prov. 1:7) The first nine chapters constitute an extended discourse on the value of wisdom; they're like an infomercial on the importance and necessity of pursuing wisdom. Wisdom leads to, and directs you how to stay on, the *path of life*, the main metaphor for the way in which God calls us to live or *walk*.

Wisdom addresses four kinds of people: the youth, the naïve, the fool and the wise man (each referred to in Proverbs 1:4-7). Proverbs is concerned with how things work, with actions and consequences, and with making distinctions among life's issues, so that our thinking and actions conform to the patterns God has irrevocably woven into life. Wisdom helps us negotiate life in the places where the rules don't readily apply. Wisdom has a handsome reward: *"For its profit is better than the profit of silver, and its gain than fine gold. She is more precious than jewels; and nothing you desire compares with her. Long life is in her right hand; in her left hand are riches and honor. Her ways are pleasant ways, all her paths are peace. She is a tree of life to those who take hold of her, and happy are all who hold her fast."* (Prov. 3:13-18) Who in their right mind wouldn't want all that! It's the American dream—long life, riches, honor, peace, happiness—but not sought in the way Americans seek it.

Wisdom generally comes to us in the form of aphorisms, that is, pithy phrases stating the rule or general principles, not absolutes. As wisdom addresses us (Prov. 1:20-22), she (Lady Wisdom) speaks principally to the *heart*. In Proverbs 3:1-8, *heart* is used three times; in the first nine chapters, *heart* is used sixteen times, and sixty-five times in the whole book! Guess where Proverbs is aiming?

This really shouldn't surprise those who have read the Bible, for the whole Bible is fundamentally addressed to the heart. What's important to God is not just doing the right thing, but doing the right thing for the right reason. The Bible always looks at motives. Christianity is not about a morally restrained heart, but a supernaturally changed heart. The Christian faith is not merely knowing the facts; you could know all the revealed facts about God, and that would qualify you to be a demon! (James 2:16) God is concerned with the heart; if there's any religion that is decidedly not impressed with formality or mere ritual, it is Christianity. The head disengaged from the heart is a cheap substitute for true biblical spirituality, as is the heart uninformed by the truth. Jesus said, *"For from within, out of the* heart *of men, proceed the evil thoughts and fornications, thefts, murders, adulteries, deeds of coveting and wickedness, as well as deceit, sensuality, envy, slander, pride and foolishness. All these evil things proceed from within and defile the man."* (Mark 7:21-23)

Think of your heart as the central command control room of your life, the engine of all you do. Biblically, the heart is a dynamic, fluid concept, integrating the emotions, desires, thoughts and understanding, and the will—each of which can be distinguished, but not separated from the other. What captures the heart captures the life! That's why Solomon tells you to learn to *write on your heart*. The question, therefore, is not, *"Are* you writing on your heart?" Rather, *"What* are you writing on your heart?" We're all scripting something for our heart to read. What should you write on your heart? The simple answer to the question is in Proverbs 3:3: *kindness and truth*. We'll get to that later. First, in order that we might become superb at writing on our hearts, there

15

are things we need to know about the heart. Years ago my wife taught calligraphy classes. She taught beginners that certain inks must be matched with certain papers, depending on their unique properties. For example, if you used the wrong ink on a certain type of paper, the ink would bleed on the paper and appear very messy. Our lives are messy when we don't write well on our hearts. You'll script something spiritually stunning when you know what to write on your heart. You'll write most effectively on your heart when you know accurately the nature of that upon which you write. What properties of the heart do you need to understand in order to write effectively upon it?

Seven things to know about your heart

1. The heart is the wellspring of life.

"Watch over your heart with all diligence, for from it flows the springs of life." (Prov. 4:23) Biblical audiences understood the vital importance of this image; springs or wells were critical to survival. The climate, dry and hot, demanded much water, both for humans and for their livestock. Since livestock were essentially their savings and retirement accounts in one, water was an integral component of their existence. If you owned a spring, you'd protect it; if your enemy wanted to kill you, the easiest way was to destroy your well. *"Like a trampled spring and a polluted well, is a righteous man who gives way before the wicked."* (Prov. 25:26)

No wonder Proverbs 4:23 commands us to guard our hearts *with all diligence*; if the spring of life becomes contaminated, the life will be ruined. No doubt, you are diligent in your pursuit of certain things in your life. That's good. *"The precious possession of a man is diligence."* (Prov. 12:27) But are you diligent for the most important thing?

2. The pulse of the heart is worship.

Psychologists often define human beings in terms of their needs. Abraham Maslow developed a hierarchy of needs, the apex of which is the need for self-actualization. Others stress the needs for significance (Am I important?) and security (Am I loved?). No doubt, these function in the human psyche; however, this is not the most accurate way to understand people. We are, by nature, most fundamentally, worshippers. God made us that way. Life in the

Garden of Eden before the entrance of sin revolved around God. Adam and Eve related to God in perfect fellowship and delight. They undoubtedly gave God His due—honor, trust, their supreme delight. Although the creation was unspoiled and unspeakably perfect, God Himself was their exceeding joy.

By "worship," we mean that the heart, by nature, esteems, treasures, desires or delights in something. Our human proclivity is to give ourselves to something. The heart is like a leech, latching on to something to draw life from it. Jesus said, *"Where your treasure is, there will your heart be also."* (Matt. 6:21) The one inexorably follows the other. Think of your heart as a magnet; one side repels, the other side draws. Once human beings fell from their status of perfect communion with God, their hearts continued to worship—but they did not worship God! Sin works in the heart so that it is simultaneously repelled from God and drawn to give its affection to something else. The Apostle Paul in Romans 1 describes this as an exchange, a trading or repelling the *true* God while worshipping or drawing to a created god.

Consider the following dynamic at work in the heart of every person. We know God because God has made Himself evident to us. *"...Because that which is known about God is evident within them; for God made it evident to them. For since the creation of the world His invisible attributes, His eternal power and divine nature, have been clearly seen, being understood through what has been made, so that they are without excuse."* (Rom. 1:19-20) We actively suppress the truth and try to shove it out of our consciousness. *"For the wrath of God is revealed from heaven against all ungodliness and unrighteousness of men, who suppress the truth in unrighteousness..."* (Rom. 1:18) God declares here that there are no true atheists! Everyone knows God; God clearly makes Himself known to all, such that *they are without excuse.* He is the truth, which we all attempt to suppress *in unrighteousness.* We see this vividly demonstrated in the alcoholic who vehemently denies he has a problem, all the while continuing to abuse alcohol. He suppresses the blatant reality of his struggle, and hides from himself that he's suppressing it.

We refuse to honor God and exchange the truth for a lie. *"For even though they knew God, they did not honor him as God, or give thanks; but they became futile in their speculations, and their foolish heart was darkened."* (Rom. 1:21) Lest we think folks are merely ignorant of God, Paul goes on to explain, *"Professing to be wise, they became fools, and exchanged the glory of the incorruptible God for an image in the form of corruptible man...for they exchanged the truth of God for a lie, and worshipped and served the creature rather than the Creator, who is blessed forever."* (Rom. 1:22-23)

Ignorance of God is no one's problem! Refusal to honor, thank and love Him is! Our hearts are ruled by a worship dynamic. We exchange God's glory for an inferior created glory. When we serve the creature, we live a lie, because the Creator alone is meant to be served. When we serve things rather than God, we inevitably become slaves of those things (which the Bible calls *idols*). We *have* to have them; they demand we give ourselves to them. That's why Paul describes the dynamic of idolatry as a downward spiraling of insensitivity to God. *"...Because of the hardness of their heart; and they, having become callous, have given themselves over to sensuality for the practice of every kind of impurity with a continual lust for more."* (Eph. 4:18-19) Our idols promise a kind of salvation or "life" (delivering us from the misery of sin) by temporarily giving us satisfaction, peace, happiness, contentment, well-being, etc. But, idols always fail us because only God is large enough to be our life and satisfaction.

Proverbs puts this particular theology in very practical terms. Given the use of the words *delight, seek, enter and rule*, Proverbs 2 depicts a pattern at work in the heart. What you *delight* in, you will *seek*; what you *seek* will *enter* you. What *enters* you will *rule* you; what *rules* you will either *enslave* or *deliver* you. Peter echoes this in 2 Peter 2:19, *"For by what a man is overcome, by this he is enslaved."* Jesus said, *"He who sins is a slave to sin."* (John 8:34)

Therefore, always think of yourself as a worshipper. At the beginning of man's creation, God wired him for worship; that hasn't changed since the Fall. Sin, however, has left man with an irresistible drive to give himself to anything *but* the Creator. A most helpful question to ask yourself is, "To what am I giving myself?" What do I believe will make me whole and happy? What is it I really delight in? Is it power, possessions, pleasure, intellectual prowess, a place of prominence, relational peace?

3. We're all born with a heart defect: a mechanism of self-justification.

Notice the dual warning of Proverbs 3:5-8. *"Don't lean on your own understanding"* (v. 5) and *"don't be wise in your own eyes"* (v. 7). Why does the text warn against this? Because it is our natural tendency to trust ourselves, *and* our natural understanding is untrustworthy (ironically!). There is no flat ground around our heart; we're always leaning on something—either ourselves or God, on our understanding or on divine revelation.

This captures the primary difference between the wise man and the fool: the fool trusts only himself and he hates reproof. *"Fools despise wisdom and instruction...hate knowledge...disdain rebuke..."* (Proverbs 1:7,22,25) The fool's theme song is, "I did it my way." His battle cry is, "Nobody tells me what to do." His creed is, "To thine own self be true." Isn't it amazing how easy it is to live that way in a free, affluent society? (Chapter 5 explores this thought.)

We are actually perpetuating foolishness in our society. The prevailing view of children in our culture is that, given a chance, they will find the right way to go. However, this notion flies in the face of biblical truth. Deuteronomy 6 tells parents to teach their children God's way, because they'll never find it naturally. Proverbs 22:15 explains this dynamic: *"Foolishness is bound up in the heart of a child."*

Foolishness resides naturally in the hearts of all people; we are born sinners. It stays there until it is removed or systematically unraveled. Notice how the following verses describe the dynamic of foolishness. *"There is a way which seems right to a man, but its end is the way of death."* (Prov. 14:12) *"Every man's way is right in his own eyes, but the Lord weighs the heart."* (Prov. 21:2) *"The way of a fool is right in his own eyes..."* (Prov. 12:15) When you add these up you have a self-deceived heart, described in Jeremiah 17:9. *"The heart is more deceitful than all else and is desperately sick; who can understand it?"* The fool is self-deceived and doesn't know it; he is constantly justifying himself.

The wise, on the contrary, seek counsel, acquire wisdom, search out God's word. Wisdom knows this truth: we are not innately well acquainted with ourselves, but with only that part of us we like. We tend to hide our worst side from ourselves. Jesus illustrated this when He said, *"Before you take the speck out of someone's eye, deal with the log in your own."* (Matt. 7:5) We have this uncanny ability to see faults in others through a lens that filters out our own faults. Then, when we do disappoint ourselves, we rationalize, blame others and realign our standards so they are essentially attainable.

Do you see that this means you simply can't write on your heart whatever you want? The government may extend to you the right to fashion your religion according to your own wishes, but God doesn't give you that right! He requires you to think accurately about Him, who He is and the world He has made. He requires you to know yourself truly, so you can know Him truly.

4. The natural heart is at war with God.

By now you may be thinking, "I'm reading this book to be encouraged, to feel good. This guy's telling me how rotten I am—no thanks!" Please hang in there. I know this is offensive. The Bible never promises to flatter anyone! Jesus said, "The *truth* will set you free." (John 8:32) The popular notion that people are basically good is completely foreign to the Bible. It stems, rather, from humanism, a decidedly anti-biblical approach to life. The Bible never tells you that in your natural condition, you're OK. If the doctor reads the lab results based on a diagnosis you can't make on your own, are you going to storm out of his office because he has tough news? Does that change the diagnosis? No, spiritual healing comes when you treat the right disease with the right remedy. Most people know they aren't perfect. But our intuitive treatment plan is either to deny we have a serious heart problem, or to try to be a better person. Neither works because neither touches the heart. Improving spiritually without going deep into the heart is like trying to cut the lawn without a blade in the mower.

God has put an illustration of this on our bodies. Can you inspect your back? Not without a mirror or a trustworthy source to tell you what it's like. I have a friend who, because he spent too much time surfing in the California sun, has skin cancers periodically surface on his back. He has his wife do regular checks to inspect what he can't see. How much more true of our hearts! We need the mirror of God's word. We need the faithful inspection of a trustworthy friend to tell us where the problems are. That's what God's word is—a mirror and a friend—to expose sin, leading us to repentance and life!

Now, are you ready to face the gruesome reality that your heart is at war with God? Where does the Bible teach that? *"He who walks in his righteousness fears the Lord, but he who is crooked in his ways* despises *Him."* (Prov. 14:2) *"The foolishness of man subverts his way, and his heart* rages *against the Lord."* (Prov. 19:3) *"The fool has said in his heart, 'There is no God.'"* (Ps. 14:1) *"For if while we were* enemies *(of God)..."* (Rom. 5:10) *"The mind set on the flesh is* hostile *toward God..."* (Rom. 8:6) These are "hard" verses, indeed! We just don't believe them at first glance, do we? Did you feel internal denial as you read them? But to deny what God clearly states is foolishness.

Foolishness is an attempt to make sense out of life without the light of the God of life. The fool insists on being his own interpreter of reality, living *as if* God is unnecessary. Why is there so little praise, affection, gratitude, sense of wonder or felt-need toward God in our hearts? It's worse than ignorance. We hate Him. We basically tell Him, "Keep your grubby hands off my life." Maybe you've never literally said that; but haven't you essentially lived that way, especially if you've never come to grips with this internal hostility toward God? Have you ever said to God, "Take me, all of me, have your way completely. I am nothing; you are everything! I submit 100% of me to 100% of you 100% of the time!" The Bible says that the war in our hearts works actively against that. Think soberly about Paul's assessment of the heart in Romans 3:10-18. *"There is none who does good, not even one; there is none who understands, none seek for God...there is no fear of God in their hearts..."*

5. Someone else is writing on your heart.

The first nine chapters of Proverbs depict a conflict between two suitors after human souls. The protagonist, Lady Wisdom, calls to us. *"Wisdom shouts in the street, she lifts her voice in the square...how long, O naïve ones, will you love simplicity? Turn to my reproof, behold, I will pour out my spirit on you, I will make my words known to you..."* (Prov. 1:20f) On the other hand, the antagonist, Dame Folly, also calls out. *"The woman of folly is boisterous, she is naïve and knows nothing...calling to those who pass by, who are making their paths straight..."* (Prov. 9:13f)

Dame Folly represents Satan, the liar and deceiver, who is calling along the path of life, "Over here, this is better, God is boring and mean, your parents are stupid, the church is for weak people, be strong in yourself, you *alone* must determine what is true for you!" We can't treat the notion of spiritual warfare in any depth here. (See chapter 17.) The point is to know that Satan is writing on your heart, but he is not writing about himself. He essentially seeks to convey two messages: distrust God and trust yourself.

6.   The heart is covered with Teflon.

I'm old enough to remember pots and pans before the marvelous invention of non-stick Teflon. Most of the time you cooked, something would stick on the bottom of the pan. Not with Teflon: easy to cook, easy to clean! Teflon-coated things were slick! You need to think of your heart that way; things don't stick. We are prone to forgetfulness, particularly in the spiritual realm. That's why Proverbs 3 begins, *"My son, do not forget my teachings."* Moses constantly urged Israel during their wilderness wanderings to both *remember* what God had done in the Exodus, and *not forget* the wonders they had witnessed. Why make such a big deal about this? Even the best truths don't easily stick to our Teflon-like hearts.

Have you ever seen a contest to determine who can do the most chin-ups or who can hang the longest in a pull-up position? Why is it so hard? The forces of gravity pull relentlessly on the weight of the body. So it is in the spiritual realm. Relentlessly pulling on our hearts are the forces of sin in this world. If not resisted, spiritual entropy will pull us toward irreparable, de-humanizing self-indulgence. For this reason, we need to write on our hearts and keep writing on them. This is not natural to us! We are accustomed to engraving special words on a silver plate, and there they stay. If only it were so easy with our hearts! But it just isn't so. Psalm 1 describes the wise man's writing on the heart. *"His delight is in the law of the Lord, and on it he meditates day and night."*

Notice how Peter doesn't hesitate to remind his readers of truths they already know. *"Therefore, I shall always be ready to remind you of these things, even though you already know them, and have been established in the truth which is present with you. And I consider it right...to stir you up by way of reminder...This is now, beloved, the second letter I am writing to you in which I am stirring your sincere mind by way of reminder."* (2 Peter 1:12,13; 3:1)

7. The heart can be changed ONLY by God's Spirit.

One final truth from Proverbs to be delineated in this chapter: we are unable to clean or change ourselves spiritually. *"Who can say, 'I have cleansed my heart, I am pure from sin?'"* (Prov. 20:9) The Bible's brute honesty about the nature of sin in us is designed to cause great desperation, a cry of helplessness, a plea for deliverance. We must come to the place where we are sure we cannot save ourselves, that we are actually our own worst enemy, and that as wonderful as God's wisdom is, even wisdom can't cure the heart. No, God alone must cleanse us by His Son and set us free from our own hearts. The promise of the Bible is that He does just that: He gives us a new heart. Proverbs 1:20-23 anticipates the coming of the Spirit to apply Christ's work to us. Lady Wisdom calls to us all. *"Turn to my reproof; behold, I will pour out my spirit on you, I will make my words known to you."*

The prophets also anticipate the Spirit's coming. *"Moreover, the Lord your God will circumcise your heart and the heart of your descendants, to love the Lord your God with all your heart and with all your soul, in order that you may live."* (Deut. 30:6) *"I will put My law within them, and on their heart I will write it; and I will be their God, and they shall be My people."* (Jeremiah 31:33) *"And I shall give them one heart, and shall put a new spirit within them. And I shall take the heart of stone out of their flesh and shall give them a heart of flesh, that they may walk in My statues and keep My ordinances..."* (Ezekiel 11:19; 36:26) These promises are fulfilled in the work of Jesus Christ, whose blood *cleanses us from all unrighteousness* (1 John 1:9) and who makes us new by the power of His Spirit. (Chapter 11 explores how this happens.)

I have sought to demonstrate that our biggest problem is our own heart. For those who admit as much, great hope resides in the heart of God: He will give you a new one through the gospel of Jesus Christ! Now we turn to Genesis to discern how God has fashioned the heart.

[24]Then God said, "Let the earth bring forth living creatures after their kind: cattle and creeping things and beasts of the earth after their kind"; and it was so. [25]And God made the beasts of the earth after their kind, and the cattle after their kind, and every thing that creeps on the ground after its kind; and God saw that it was good. [26]Then God said, "Let us make man in our image, according to Our likeness; and let them rule over the fish of the sea and over the birds of the sky and over the cattle and over all the earth, and over every creeping thing that creeps on the earth." [27]And God created man in His own image, in the image of God He created him; male and female He created them.

Genesis 1:24-27

The Heart's Purpose: Reflecting His Image

"You will inevitably pursue whatever your heart thinks life should be."

In 1973, John Lennon struck gold with his best selling song *Imagine*:

> *Imagine there's no heaven, it's easy if you try,*
> *No hell below us, above us only sky.*
> *Imagine all the people, living for today.*
>
> *Imagine there's no countries, it isn't hard to do,*
> *Nothing to kill or die for, no religion, too.*
> *Imagine all the people, living life in peace.*
>
> *Imagine there's no possessions, I wonder if you can,*
> *No need for greed or hunger, a brotherhood of man.*
> *Imagine all the people, sharing all the world.*
>
> *You may say I'm a dreamer, but I'm not the only one,*
> *I hope someday you'll join us, and the world will be as one.*

What is this? Isn't this the cry of the human heart for a perfect world? Isn't this a yearning for the full goodness of life: peace and brotherhood, without the scourge of hunger, death, greed or conflict? You could write your own script for paradise; sometimes you go there daydreaming, or maybe you travel to Disney World! Why do we long for this? Why does a notion of paradise linger deep in the human psyche? After all, we don't need paradise to survive. This yearning transcends mere existence; as far as we know, animals don't yearn for this kind of stuff! How do we account for this desire?

Genesis 1 tells us we were made for paradise. Though now fallen, outside of paradise, and tainted by sin, our hearts still bear the evidence of our original creation in the Garden of Eden, bearing the image of God. That's why everyone has a vision or an internal sense of what life should be. Why is that so important? Because you inevitably will pursue whatever you think life should be. It's true for us, as it was true for the original audience of Genesis.

Moses is writing Genesis to the newly formed covenant community of God's people delivered fresh out of four hundred years of bondage in Egypt. Their identity, sense of life and purpose had been determined by the culture in which they lived. Now God wants them to understand the true purpose for their existence—as He does you! What does Genesis tell us about the true purpose of life? It's pretty clear and simple: God made everything, by His own power and for His own purpose. He fashioned from nothing a perfect world, made man and set him in it to enjoy it forever. Without that foundational principle, human beings never find true purpose. But, there's a critical component at the heart of the goodness of life. It's found in the verses we read. What makes life good? We catch it in the drama of the creation account:

God shapes His creation using a process of separation or differentiation (borrowing from Frances Schaeffer, *Genesis in Time and Space*):

Light	separated from	darkness	=	days	
Water above heavens	separated from	water below	=	expanse	in
Land	separated from	water below	=	earth and seas	
Non-life	separated from	life on earth	=	vegetation	
Lights for day	separated from	lights for night	=	sun, moon, stars	
Animals on earth	separated from	life in sea and air	=	two animal kingdoms	

At each step, God evaluates His handiwork: *"it was good."* But at Genesis 1:26, the cadence changes to *"Let us."* The Divine Counsel acts *personally* to form man, rather than *"let there be."* God separates human life from all other life as an act of special creation. Man is formed from the dust. He comes to life by the breath of God. He is stamped with the divine image. Now it's *very good*! If the trees could talk, we might hear them evaluate everything being made around them: "good...good...good." But once Adam and Eve were created, their assessment would have been "*Wow*! Look at them, a reflection of the invisible God! There's *nothing* else like them!" It is as if you brought everything you value and placed it on the floor in your living room; there in the midst of all your treasures (car keys, jewelry, special antiques, graduate school diploma, etc.), sits your child. As good and beautiful or costly and significant as all that stuff may be, there's no comparison between things and your own offspring.

That's what Genesis tells us about God's evaluation of human life. Human beings occupy a special place in the heart of God because they alone bear His image. That is what makes human life good—the image of God. Songs, movies and books that call us to imagine human perfection raise a critical question: What in fact makes life good? Your vision of the good life is debilitatingly deficient until it revolves around the *imago dei*, the image of God, the stamp of God's glory upon His special creations.

What is the image of God?

One way to think about it is in terms of source and function.

Source: The image of God separates man from all the other creatures. Humans do not possess inherent dignity. Our worth or value is derived or dependent upon the image of God. A secular worldview cannot assign dignity to a group of evolved *Homo sapiens*. They are merely one group of amassed molecules in the midst of a billion others. God's evaluation gives us glory and honor: we *alone* are made in God's image. It is also cause for humility and dependence: we are *only* in the image, we aren't God, and remain utterly dependent upon Him for our very breath. (Acts 17:25)

Function: God created man to rule. We bear the image of the king of creation as His vice-regents to rule the creation. God said,

"Have dominion, it's all for you. Use it well, wisely, as stewards of my creation. It's Mine, but you can enjoy it." God also created man to reflect God's image. As God's image bearers, we are called to reflect His attributes to the rest of creation, much as a mirror reflects an object distinct from itself. The effect is that anything in creation could look upon man and marvel, "Stunning, now I see something of what God is like, an approximation of uncreated glory, a reflection of the divine being."

This glory is especially evident in three distinct elements of being human: morality—man has true knowledge, righteousness and holiness; spirituality—man has a soul; personality—man is capable of rational thought, feeling and volition. That's why God requires the protection of innocent human life. Murder is an attack on the image of God. So serious is an assault on the image, that God says an offender should be put to death. After the flood, God instituted capital punishment along this line of reasoning. *"Whoever sheds man's blood, by man his blood shall be shed, for in the image of God he made them."* (Gen. 9:6) James 3:9 requires you to honor the image in how you speak to another. *"With the tongue we bless our Lord and Father; and with it we curse men, who have been made in the likeness of God."*

What is the evidence fallen creatures still bear God's image?

When we look at what human hearts long for and seem to intrinsically value, we see fossils or imprints in the soul of many aspects of life in the Garden of Eden, life where we reflected God's image perfectly. Consider the following.

1. We long for that perfect person.

In Genesis, God determined that Adam and Eve would *"become one flesh."* (Gen. 2:24) Among other things, that meant they were astoundingly well suited for each other. They lacked nothing that could be experienced in the glory of human relationship. The longing to be loved, esteemed, cherished, nourished, appreciated, valued, understood—it was all there.

Emotional, physical, intellectual and spiritual oneness pulsed through their union. And don't we all still long for that? Isn't she always looking for Mr. Right? Doesn't he have a picture in his mind of the "one sent from heaven, made especially for me?" Think about the lyrics to virtually every love song. Don't they extol the height of human bliss expressed in love for another?

2.   We esteem the excellent.

God made the garden so that *"every tree is pleasing to the sight."* (Gen. 2:9) Nothing could have improved the physical environment of the creation. It was pristine, excellent, unsurpassed in perfect function and aesthetics. After all, God made it; His handiwork bears the stamp of His own unspeakable excellence and creative genius. The human heart, though now far removed from that idyllic place, still bears the imprint of it. We love the excellent—in sports, the arts, music. Musicologists tell us that the experience of superior music can actually hurt because the music transports the soul to paradise—that for which heart longs but doesn't have.

3.   We desire to live in a perfect environment.

"God put them in the Garden." (Gen. 2:9) We were made for perfection, and our hearts still know it. Think about it: why do we hate to think about death, shudder at a tornado, become annoyed with ants and bee stings and drought and sunburn? We weren't made for those things! God gave Adam and Eve a "beer that tastes great" *and* it was "less filling!" In Eden, they were safe, free from threats, poverty, calamity. They were in control of their world, under God's kind Lordship. They were created to live forever. God has *set eternity in the heart of man.* (Eccl. 3:11)

4.   We long for existence without pain.

"And God blessed them." (Gen. 1:28) The blessings of God meant fullness of life and purpose without the presence of suffering, angst or breakdown of any kind in the order of all things. Why are two enormous industries in the U.S. centered on preserving youthfulness and alleviating pain? We bear in our hearts

the fossil of the original creation—painless existence. Don't people commit suicide because there is supposedly less pain in death?

5. We recognize aesthetic and moral goodness.

God said, *"Behold, it was very good."* (Gen. 1:31) If this world merely consists of molecules in motion, as the secularist's faith would have us believe, then how do we account for this innate sense of justice we all feel? How does Hollywood, with its self-admitted godless worldview, account for movies that extol goodness, friendship, justice and kindness? These are all virtues that only make sense within a God-centered worldview. We know why. We understand why people are concerned about the environment, the abuse of power in government and corporations that lie and cheat. These things make sense only when we see that God's imprint of goodness is still pounded upon our hearts.

How is the image restored?

All is not well with the image of God. Yes, we still bear it *structurally* in some fashion as I've just tried to demonstrate, but certainly not in the way God intended it *functionally*. What happened? Sin. Adam and Eve beat John Lennon to the punch. Did you notice the striking difference between Lennon's paradise and the Bible's? The presence of God! How like fallen creatures to desire the paradise of God without the God of paradise! This is our most basic problem: wanting everything God made but on our own terms, without the blessing of the presence of God. We are fairly blatant about it in our country; it's called the American dream: peace, pleasure, possessions, prosperity—but without concern to reflect the glory of God, to adorn God's moral beauty in our hearts, or to enjoy them within the limits of God's law.

If you desire to fulfill your true purpose, you need a power beyond yourself to transform your heart. That's what Jesus promises to do for all who call upon Him for grace. It's His pleasure to restore your heart to its proper function; He does so by His Spirit. How? He does so as you admit you've spoiled the image by living for yourself and not God's glory. Then admit your heart needs cleansing, and no amount of good works can clean your heart of the stain of sin—that would be like trying to remove three coats of thick paint with water and a toothbrush. Finally, go to Jesus Christ for cleansing and forgiveness. He came to take upon His beautiful image everything that defiles yours. The sin that would have destroyed you devastated Him on the cross.

When you seek Christ in this kind of humility, you can be certain of two things. One, He always meets you. Two, a marvelous heart transformation has begun.

[18]And we all, with unveiled face beholding as in a mirror the glory of the Lord, are being transformed into the same image from glory to glory, just as from the Lord, the Spirit.

2 Corinthians 3:18

Stages of Heart Transformation

"Spiritual transformation is normally gradual."

Have you ever seen someone change significantly? Have you witnessed an authentic before-and-after radical transformation that left you in awe? One of the greatest joys in pastoral ministry is watching God change people and hearing the testimonies of those He changes. You see newness in their countenance, priorities and passions; you see new zeal for truth, goodness and faithfulness. I'll always cherish the account of a successful business owner in Charlottesville, VA who described how he once would *never* miss a golf outing on Sunday morning, but now would *never* miss the pleasure of church on Sunday morning. God really changes people!

Almost everyone has read about the conversion of the Apostle Paul. So famous is it that we've coined a phrase to describe such dramatic change: a Damascus Road experience (because Paul was literally on the road to Damascus when Jesus personally changed him, Acts 9). Sometimes people change dramatically *from Saul to Paul*. Normally, however, spiritual transformation happens gradually, step-by-step, usually in fits and starts.

While not everyone changes for the same reason or in the same way, it is possible to make a general paradigm for spiritual transformation. This chapter explores such a paradigm. It certainly doesn't apply in all cases, but it may give you various benchmarks to help you ask, "Where am I with respect to where God wants me?" It is very much like building a house. Working from a master plan, an architect's blue prints, the builder starts at the foundation and builds in consecutive stages until the finished product mirrors the original design. It is fairly easy to tell where a house is in comparison to the final product. Just as it takes time to build a house, so it takes time to *reconstruct* a human being after the image of Christ. That is the goal of our salvation: Christ-likeness. *"For whom He foreknew, He also predestined to become conformed to the image of His Son, that He might be the first-born among many brethren."* (Rom. 8:29) *"...You have put on the new self who is being renewed to a true knowledge according to the image of the One who created him..."* (Col. 3:10)

When a person sees the wonder and glory of what he can become in Christ, he tends to want it quickly. We are, after all, the microwave generation. God, however, doesn't work that way. If He wants a squash, then yes, that takes about 90 days. But when God produces a towering oak tree, He takes 90 years. An American tourist asked a resident of a quaint Swiss village, "Were any famous people born here?" "No," the resident replied, "just babies." We're all born babes in Christ. We grow by baby steps. A little boy stood next to the enormous slab of marble upon which a sculptor worked. He asked the man what he was sculpting. "A horse," he replied! "How do you do that?" asked the boy. "I chip away everything from the block that isn't horse." God has a lot to chip off of us that isn't Christ. It takes time. It is painful. But God is also merciful: He doesn't allow us to see all at once the horrifying extent of wickedness in our hearts.

What follows is a description of stages of spiritual transformation. You might call it a yardstick for appetites. Where God wants us is *"tasting and seeing that the Lord is good."* (Ps. 34) But like the child who is sick, there is no appetite where there is no health. As we heal, our appetite increases. Healthy spirituality exists where we hunger for God, are satisfied in Him, and savor and enjoy His fellowship. We know *"Christ is our all in all"* (Col. 3:11) when nothing we desire compares with Him. But that isn't where any of us begins spiritually. We have appetites for many other things. So what must happen for us to desire Christ more than anything else?

We must experience a process of internal transformation of appetite. Here is one way to depict that process.

Yardstick for spiritual appetites

Stage 1: self-satisfied. We are born naturally complacent toward the things of God. We simply won't move toward Him. Our way seems best to us. We live autonomously in a mode of self-justification (explored in the previous chapters). We are deceived to our true spiritual condition. We are "full but empty."

Stage 2: spiritually empty. At this point, something happens in life, which causes us to ask questions. "What's it all about? Why am I here?" Perhaps due to suffering or loss, we sense that things don't add up, we feel a lack of purpose. "This isn't the life I hoped for or dreamt about." Perhaps failure has tainted our former optimism; perhaps success has left us longing for more. Often a crisis in relationships breeds loneliness, fear or rejection. This emptiness is a very good thing: when life isn't working, perhaps God is.

Stage 3: spiritually hungry. This stage naturally follows the previous one. What's the difference? At this point, we experience weakness. Our props fail us; our methods of coping begin to misfire. Our default mode becomes self-destructive. It hits us afresh: my weaknesses are too strong for me, and my strengths are too weak for me. We conclude, rightly, it isn't all about me. I must begin to take God seriously. So a new humility is born: there is an agenda in life larger than mine is! My soul is too big to be filled with all the pleasures I have sought.

Stage 4: hungry for personal knowledge. Now I'm convinced that life is more than mere matter. God made everything, He made me and I want to know Him. No longer can I be content knowing about God, or going through religious motions to feel good about myself. God must be a glorious person, and I've been indifferent to Him. God doesn't exist to serve me; I am created to serve Him. Since that is true, I can no longer be in control of my spirituality.

It's either God's way or a false way. Therefore, I long for revelation from God about Himself. I've starved my soul on my imagination's concoctions of what God is like. Now it is time to hear from God in His word, the Bible.

Stage 5: convicted of sin. As we meet God in His revelation, we realize He is a person we have harmed, He has a heart we have grieved, He has standards we have spurned. Thus, we meet ourselves in a new way. We can no longer pass off moral lapses as mistakes or judgment errors; we are guilty, we have sinned.

This is a very critical juncture in spiritual transformation. Our pride wants to try to clean things up in our own strength. We want to *do* to compensate for what has been *done*. We think it is right to pay for our wrongs by reforming ourselves, by balancing the scales of morality. Which direction will we go? Will we merely reform by turning over a new leaf, and become moralists, or will we seek a refuge? The moralist repents of his sins, but the Christian repents of his sins *and* his self-righteousness (his attempts to curry God's favor or to establish his own righteousness).

Stage 6: hungry for forgiveness. This is the stage where sin weighs heavily. Sin is more than doing wrong; we feel the need to be forgiven. Sin stands between God and me. We know our efforts at self-improvement can't make us clean. *"If thou, O Lord, should mark iniquities, who could stand?"* (Ps. 130:1) Now, sin is more than simply my failure, putting me at some disadvantage. It is an affront to God. Sin isn't simply breaking the rules; it is breaking God's heart. I understand that God, amazingly, provides the only refuge from the condemnation of sin in His beloved Son, Jesus Christ.

Stage 7: hungry for righteousness. The sweetness of forgiveness and the consciousness of sin's odiousness produce a desire to be much more like Christ. But it's not in me to be that. Who will plead my case? Is there someone else who can live in my place? I need absolute, unwavering moral perfection in order to make a claim on the holy presence of God. The gospel tells me I have that as a gift through faith in Christ. Once I ask Jesus to save me from my sins, He promises to bear the penalty of sin for me by His death on the cross, and to credit to me His perfect righteousness. All I need to stand in the presence of a holy God is accomplished by Christ, and given as a gift of grace.

Stage 8: resting in faith. All that the Bible reveals that Jesus is for me brings peace. Faith makes me believe God will deal bountifully with me, in spite of myself. I now understand that my sin is a sin against love, and that most sin is motivated by a doubt in the goodness of God.

Stage 9: serving, praising, enjoying. Here is where God wants us to be. This is the good life. This is life on earth in its fullest. We experience wonder and awe before God, though not perfectly or as we shall one day in glory. We learn to fill our souls with Him. Now we deeply believe that nothing we desire compares with Him. And yet there is a paradox: in this state; we still thirst for God. Yes, we are content, but certainly not complacent. We will also find ourselves cycling back through these stages at periods in our life. We are slow to change!

Although this paradigm doesn't fit everyone's experience, it may help you gauge what's happening in your heart. Wherever you are, Christ promises to meet you and to move you gently toward the next stage. All that is necessary He will provide by His grace. All who wait upon Him will find their strength renewed. All who seek Him will assuredly find Him!

We turn next to examine the place our hearts engage with this world: the path of life.

26He who trusts in his own heart is a fool, but he who walks wisely will be delivered.

Proverbs 28:26

The Path a Healthy Heart Finds

"Wisdom takes the guesswork out of finding the path to life."

Robert Frost begins his famous poem:

> "Two roads diverged in a yellow wood,
> And sorry I could not travel both
> And be one traveler, long I stood
> And looked down one, as far I could…"

And ends it:

> "I took the one less traveled by
> And that has made all the difference."

The tension momentarily created by Robert Frost in his poem's beginning—which of two roads to take—is resolved by poem's end on the happy note: the one traveled "made all the difference." What a wonderful way to end a journey, or, for that matter, your life! But how do we know which road to take? Which involves the least risk or affords the greatest opportunity? Suppose you stood at the edge of the life's "yellow wood," knowing that the two paths led in very different directions to extremely different destinations: one led to paradise, the other to eternal torment. Would you wander nonchalantly forward on a blissful journey, or would you want to *know* which road to take? The poet seemed to choose by chance. Would you?

You do, in fact, stand at the crossroads of two divergent roads. Solomon employed similar imagery in Proverbs long before Robert

Frost. Why? Because when a teacher needs to communicate something of tremendous importance, he uses the familiar and the vivid. Everyone in the Ancient Near East used roads and paths everyday, just as we today use roads and sidewalks. Thus, people in any time or culture can readily imagine the metaphor. Proverbs likens life to the path, the road, the way, the highway. Presumably, you should be thinking about where you're ultimately going as often as you use one!

How do you know which path will lead you to paradise and not to hell? Isn't the point of the divergent path that you can't see the end? After all, there aren't large, green highway signs in the spiritual realm. The path is one of the concerns of wisdom, the theme of Proverbs. Proverbs 1 addresses four types of people (you are tacitly invited to determine which one you are): the fool, who needs a major moral overhaul; the naïve, who needs wisdom; the youth, who lacks experience; and the wise person, who relishes instruction, correction and observation. Wisdom is concerned with making distinctions, comparing things, and with the way things work. Wisdom understands that this is God's world and He governs it according to certain immutable principles. The Proverbs are addressed to a son from his father, indicating the covenantal nature of revelation: what God reveals is meant to be obeyed. The sayings of wisdom typically are aphorisms; that is, they are pithy statements that are true as a rule, yet cannot be absolutized. The wise find the path of life, avoid the path leading to destruction and negotiate all the dangers along the way. In broad terms, Proverbs is help for both *finding* the path of life and *negotiating* it safely.

What do you need to know in order to find the path of life?

1. There are two main paths.

"So you will walk in the way of good men, *and keep to the* paths of the righteous." (Prov. 2:20) *"Discretion will guard you, understanding will watch over you, to deliver you from* the way of evil...*from those who leave the paths of uprightness, to walk in the*

ways of darkness...*whose* paths are crooked.*" (Prov. 2:11-15)
Notice the two paths: the path of uprightness or the righteous,
also called the *path of life* (Prov. 2:19), compared with the path
of darkness, the way of evil, the *"tracks which lead to the dead"*
(Prov. 2:18).

Proverbs seems to portray all individuals starting along the
same road, needing to choose which path they will follow. There
must be a deliberate movement to the path of life; no one is on it
by default. The need for a decisive choice is accentuated by two
voices calling out from beside the road. *"Wisdom shouts in the
street, she lifts her voice in the square; at the head of the noisy
streets she cries out; at the entrance of the gates of the city she
utters her sayings..."* (Prov. 1:20-21) Even before we meet
Lady Wisdom, the protagonist of Proverbs, we are warned about
the voice of an antagonist. *"My son, if* sinners *entice you, do not
consent. If they say, 'Come with us...' "* (Prov. 1:10)

The competition between Lady Wisdom and Dame Folly
intensifies by the conclusion of the prologue to Proverbs
(Chapters 1-9), as both call out to passersby. *"Wisdom has built
her house...she calls from the tops of the heights of the city:
Whoever is naïve, let him turn in here...forsake your folly and
live, and proceed in the way of understanding."* (Prov. 9:1-6)
*"The woman of folly is boisterous, she is naïve, and knows
nothing. And she sits at the doorway of her house, on a seat by
the high places of the city, calling to those who pass by, who are
making their paths straight: Whoever is naïve, let him turn in
here..."* (Prov. 9:13-16) Did you notice that both call from their
house, appealing to the naïve, and that Dame Folly is calling to
those who are *making their paths straight?* These are people
who want to do the right thing, but she's there tempting them.
One of the most notable embodiments of this temptation is the
adulteress. *"The lips of an adulteress drip honey, and smoother
than oil is her speech; but in the end she is bitter as wormwood,
sharp as a two-edged sword. Her feet go down to death, her*

41

steps lay hold of Sheol. She does not ponder the path of life; her ways are unstable, she does not know it." (Prov. 5:3-6)

It is no accident that the would-be seducer is superficially attractive; sin always presents its prettiest face. (Plus, physical beauty is no indicator of moral glory.) But one doesn't necessarily realize the danger until *the end*. Dating her may *taste sweet* initially, but eventually it leads to death. She takes a casual approach to life, a live-for-the-moment creed, not bothering to ponder the path of life, not knowing where she's going (in obvious contrast to the wise person who does!). The fact that Dame Folly is attractive and *talks a good talk* means we need wisdom to see beyond appearances to true intentions.

To summarize, Proverbs portrays two paths and two voices. But that's not all. The sage entertains no thoughts of moral relativism (for example, the popular but erroneous idea that "it doesn't matter which path you take since they all lead to God"), for there are also two distinct ends: death and life. *"Assuredly, the evil man will not go unpunished, but the descendants of the righteous will be delivered."* (Prov. 11:21)

Finding the right path is, therefore, a matter of life and death. *"A man who wanders from the way of understanding will rest in the assembly of the dead."* (Prov. 21:16) *"He who pursues righteousness and loyalty finds life, righteousness and honor."* (Prov. 21:21) David prays to Yahweh to *"lead me in the way everlasting."* (Ps. 139:24) Jesus contrasted the dramatic ends of the two paths with these words: *"Enter by the narrow gate; for the gate is wide, and the way is broad that leads to destruction, and many are those who enter by it. For the gate is small, and the way is narrow that leads to life, and few are those who find it."* (Matt. 7:13-14)

Proverbs is seeking to eliminate for the reader any guesswork in determining which path to follow! To increase the gravity of the choice, the sage determines that each of us know that we live in a moral universe. God, in other words, makes His evaluation of the paths. *"For the ways of a man are before the eyes of the Lord, and He watches all his paths."* (Prov. 5:21) *"The perverse in heart are an abomination to the Lord, but the blameless in their walk is His delight."* (Prov. 11:20) *"Lying lips are an abomination to the Lord, but those who deal faithfully are His delight."* (Prov. 12:22)

The wise man clings to the promise that he could be a *delight to the Lord*, the *summa bonum* of human experience.

2. We will never find the path of life on our own.

Proverbs makes no attempt to flatter human beings. It uncompromisingly indicts man's natural blindness to the right way. He thinks he knows the way, but without divine intervention or revelation, he only deceives himself. *"There is a way which seems right to a man, but its end is the way of death."* (Prov. 14:12; 16:25) How ironic! The path that *seems* right is the wrong one!

"All the ways of a man are clean in his own sight, but the Lord weighs the motives." (Prov. 16:2) Only God knows our deepest motives. *"Every man's way is right in his own eyes, but the Lord weighs the hearts."* (Prov. 21:2) We innately cut ourselves slack; we hide our motives from ourselves! *"There is a kind who is pure in his own eyes, yet is not washed from his filthiness."* (Prov. 30:12)

You have to feel guilty before you can know you're guilty! Since this is true—we simply don't get it spiritually (in the New Testament Jesus called this *"loving the darkness rather than the light,"* being blind, or being spiritually dead)—the way out of our self-deceived self-confidence is to admit our folly and forsake it for the *"fear of the Lord."* *"The fear of the Lord is the beginning of knowledge; fools despise wisdom and instruction."* (Prov. 1:7) *"Forsake your folly and live, and proceed in the way of understanding."* (Prov. 9:6) *"He who trusts in his own heart is a fool, but he who walks wisely will be delivered."* (Prov. 28:26)

To *forsake folly* is to stop trusting your own heart, leaning on your emotions, depending on your own interpretation of reality, and start admitting that you need God's revelation in order to understand God's world. If *"the fear of the Lord is the beginning of wisdom"* (Prov. 9:10), then the beginning of the fear of the Lord is the confession that you cannot save yourself, nor can wisdom. Your foolishness is rebellion against God; the need for wisdom proves you guilty and helpless to deliver yourself from sin. Therefore, the fear of the Lord should drive you to the Savior, Jesus Christ. In Christ, sinners are delivered from the penalty of foolishness and are given power by the Spirit to grow in the fear of the Lord.

This He gives through wisdom, personified as Lady Wisdom in the prologue of Proverbs. She presents herself as more desirable than anything else, as incomparably valuable. *"She is more precious than jewels; and nothing you desire compares with her."* (Prov. 3:15) *"For wisdom is better than jewels; and all desirable things can not compare with her."* (Prov. 8:11) Only Lady Wisdom has the knowledge to direct us to the right path. *"For if you cry for discernment, lift your voice for understanding; if you seek her as silver, and search for her as for hidden treasures; then you will discern the fear of the Lord, and discover the knowledge of God."* (Prov. 2:3-5) *"She is a tree of life to those who take hold of her, and happy are all who hold her fast."* (Prov. 3:18) Lady Wisdom prefigures the Lord Jesus Christ, *"in whom are hidden all the treasures of wisdom and knowledge."* (Col. 2:3) *"By his doing you are in Christ Jesus, who became for us wisdom from God, and righteousness and sanctification, and redemption..."* (1 Cor. 1:30) As we search the Old Testament for the truly wise man, for the one who fears the Lord perfectly and walks wholeheartedly in the way of wisdom, who is never seduced into false paths, we find no one who qualifies, not even Solomon, the wisest man in the world—no one until we meet Jesus in the New Testament.

Once we commit to God as the source of wisdom concerning the path, we are in a position to learn from Lady Wisdom how to negotiate the path of life. Just because one is on it does not mean he is out of danger. Along the way are many snares, divergent paths and would-be suitors to draw us aside.

3. You can never hurt yourself on the path.

"In the path of righteousness is life, and in its pathway there is no death." (Prov. 12:28) This is a critical affirmation because the heart of man doubts that following God is truly best. We believe the lie that somehow God will orchestrate calamity in our lives if we follow Him. How else do we account for our reluctance to seek Him with our whole hearts? We see what sin does to our relationship to God in the Garden after Adam and Eve fell; they were hiding from God, the One who is the perfection of love and friendship!

What do you need to know to negotiate the path of life?

1. Just as a healthy body needs food, a healthy heart needs instruction.

"He will die for lack of instruction, and in the greatness of his folly he will go astray." (Prov. 5:23) *"He who is on the path of life heeds instruction, but he who forsakes reproof goes astray."* (Prov. 10:17) Notice the explicit warning of the consequences of not listening to God. *"And you groan at your latter end, when your flesh and your body are consumed; and you say, 'How I have hated instruction! And my heart spurned reproof! And I have no listened to the voice of my teachers, nor inclined my ear to my instructors! I was almost in ruin in the midst of the assembly and congregation.'"* (Prov. 5:11-14)

2. Since we are prone to slide into error, we value rebuke.

"For the commandment is a lamp; and the teaching is a light; and reproofs for discipline are the way of life." (Prov. 6:23) *"A wise son accepts his father's discipline, but a scoffer does not listen to rebuke."* (Prov. 13:1) One test, therefore, to see if you

are on the path is how you respond to criticism. Healthy reasoning sounds like this: "Tell me if I'm wrong because I need to know. If I'm wrong, I need to change; that's far better than being wrong! If it turns out I'm not wrong, how could there be any harm in you warning me?"

3.   We are mindful of other paths luring our hearts away, and so we carefully guard the heart.

"Do not let your heart turn aside to her ways, do not stray into her paths." (Prov. 7:25) *"Watch over your heart with all diligence, for from it flow the springs of life...let your eyes look directly ahead, and let your gaze be fixed straight ahead of you. Watch the path of your feet, and all your ways will be established."* (Prov. 4:23-26) *"The highway of the upright is to depart from evil; he who watches his way preserves his life."* (Prov. 16:17)

At the same time, the wise recognize how the fool refuses to watch his path soberly. *"The way of the wicked is like darkness; they do not know over what they stumble."* (Prov. 4:19) *"She (the adulteress) does not ponder the path of life; her ways are unstable, she does not know it."* (Prov. 5:6) *"So they* [the naïve ones who refused when wisdom called, did not want her reproof, hated knowledge, did not choose the fear of the Lord, would not accept wisdom's counsel, spurned her reproof] *shall eat the fruit of their own way, and be satiated with their own devices. For the waywardness of the naïve shall kill them, and the complacency of fools shall destroy them."* (Prov. 1:31-32)

Notice the judicial hardening (a theological term for God judging sin by allowing that sin to dominate and destroy the person) that occurs: God gives the fool over to his own ways. This means, in the end, contrary to what we think, we don't *do sin*; rather, *sin does us.* We don't break God's commands, as much as we break ourselves upon them. *"His own iniquities will capture the wicked, and he will be held by the cords of his own sin."* (Prov. 5:22) *"For by what a man is overcome, to that he is enslaved."* (2 Peter 2:19) *"Truly, truly, I say to you, everyone who commits sin is a slave to sin."* (John 8:34) *"Therefore God gave them over in the lusts of their hearts to impurity..."* (Rom. 1:24)

The only reason people don't sin more is the common grace of God restraining the full extent of sin in their hearts. When God *gives us over* to our sin, He says in effect, "If you want that so badly, then you can have it, all of it." That state will destroy a human being because sin is never satisfied. *"...And they, having become callous, have given themselves over to sensuality for the practice of every kind of impurity with a continual lust for more."* (Eph. 4:19)

4. We watch diligently for the multitude of snares along the way.

Snares, such as bad company. *"Do not associate with a man given to anger; or go with a hot-tempered man, lest you learn his ways, and find a snare for yourself."* (Prov. 22:24-25) *"He who walks with wise men will be wise, but the companion of fools will suffer harm."* (Prov. 13:20) Or the fear of man—*"The fear of man brings a snare, but he who trusts in the Lord will be exalted."* (Prov. 29:25) Perhaps we run into the snare of wealth. *"Keep deception and lies far from me, give me neither poverty nor riches; feed me with the food that is my portion, lest I be full and deny thee and say, 'Who is the Lord?', or lest I be in want and steal, and profane the name of my God."* (Prov. 29:8-9) Or unchecked desires—*"Have you found honey? Eat only what you need, lest you have it in excess and vomit."* (Prov. 25:16) *"Like a city that is broken into and without walls, is a man who has no control over his spirit."* (Prov. 25:28) *"He who loves pleasure will become a poor man; he who loves wine and oil will not become rich."* (Prov. 21:16) *"A man of great anger shall bear the penalty, for if you rescue him, you will only have to do it again."* (Prov. 19:19)

Words can sometimes be a snare. *"If you have been* snared *by the words of your mouth…"* (Prov. 6:2) Unconfessed sin in a hardened heart is a snare. *"He who conceals his transgressions will not prosper, but he who confesses and forsakes them will find compassion. How blessed is the man who fears always, but he who hardens his heart will fall into calamity."* (Prov. 28:13-14) Illicit sexual pleasure is a snare. *"For the lips of an adulteress drip honey, and smoother than oil is her speech; but in the end she is bitter as wormwood, sharp as a two-edged sword."* (Prov. 5:3-4) Amongst repeated warnings in the Proverbs prologue is an extended treatment of the dangers of sex outside of God's ordaining, the marriage covenant. Chapter 7, for example, reads like an anatomy of seduction. An additional, briefer discourse is taken up in 5:1-14, with a depiction of God's alternative in verses 15-23, what might be called "the lasting delight of a faithful marriage."

5.   The path increasingly becomes self-validating.

"But the path of the righteous is like the dawn, that shines brighter and brighter until the full day." (Prov. 4:18) This verse gives great hope to those on the path, slugging it out with sin and detractors. It seems to promise that the longer we are faithful to the path, the clearer we will see what is right and how distasteful evil really is. When we start the walk of life, we love our sin too much. We feel too comfortable with the darkness; righteousness may feel odd while sin seems so normal. But as we keep to the path, like the sun increasingly illuminating the earth, the path appears less fuzzy and clearer. We long for the light of God's revelation so we won't stumble in the darkness. God's law may not make sense at first, but as we continue to walk in its light, it proves, according to the description of Psalm 19, to *"restore the soul, make wise the simple, rejoice the heart, enlighten the eyes, be more desirable than gold and sweeter than the drippings of the honey comb."*

6. We learn to trust ourselves less and trust a sovereign God more.

"In all your ways acknowledge Him and He will make your paths straight." (Prov. 3:6) *"The Lord has made everything for its own purpose..."* (Prov. 16:4) *"The mind of man plans his way, but the Lord directs his steps."* (Prov. 16:9) *"Man's steps are ordained by the Lord, how then can man understand his way?"* (Prov. 20:24) *"The horse is prepared for the day of battle, but victory belongs to the Lord."* (Prov. 21:31)

7. We learn to yield ourselves to God's plans instead of our own.

"Commit your works to the Lord, and your plans will be established." (Prov. 16:3) *"Many are the plans in a man's heart, but the counsel of the Lord, it will stand."* (Prov. 19:21) Our response to the providential workings of God is faith. Hence, we grow in the ability to trust God. *"Trust in the Lord with all your heart, and do not lean on your own understanding. In all your ways acknowledge Him, and* He will make your paths straight." (Prov. 3:5-6) Our final confidence is that God *will make our paths straight*...and that makes all the difference!

¹Then it happened in the spring, at the time when kings go out to battle, that David sent Joab and his servants with him and all Israel, and they destroyed the sons of Ammon and besieged Rabbah. But David stayed at Jerusalem. ²Now when evening came David arose from his bed and walked around on the roof of the king's house, and from the roof he saw a woman bathing; and the woman was very beautiful in appearance. ³So David sent and inquired about this woman. And one said, "Is this not Bathsheba, the daughter of Eliam, the wife of Uriah the Hittite?" ⁴And David sent messengers and took her, and when she came to him, he lay with her; and when she had purified herself from her uncleanness, she returned to her house. ⁵And the woman conceived; and she sent and told David, and said, "I am pregnant."

2 Samuel 11:1-5

A Case Study: Underestimating the Heart

"Your greatest threat is what you don't admit to yourself."

I began a sermon to college students with a series of questions. Do you believe terrorism is a real threat to our nation's security? Is it right for the government to do something about terrorism? Would it be foolish not to pursue "homeland security"? The students obviously answered these questions in the affirmative. Then I asked, "What is your greatest threat here on the college campus?" I posed a few possibilities: the West Nile virus, terrorism, academic failure, your computer crashing. Next, I asked, *"If* you knew the greatest threat to your welfare, would you do something about it?" The obvious answer, again, would be in the affirmative. I then made the bold claim that the greatest threat to their welfare was spiritual. In fact, the safer things are physically or environmentally, the greater the danger spiritually.

Let me explain from the life of David. Most people know the story of David's great sin with Bathsheba. What they may not know are the conditions that surrounded it. We live in an age, unlike David's, of unprecedented personal freedom and affluence. Never before in the history of the world has a culture afforded so many of its members the plethora of pleasures, entertainments, opportunities and the like to satisfy its cravings for sensuality, power and comfort. In a sense, we each are enabled to have our own little kingdoms. In that regard, we stand in very similar shoes with King David. He had ample opportunity to satisfy his cravings for sensuality, power and comfort. The reason he failed through adultery and murder, I believe, is he did not deal honestly with his greatest threat: his *heart's attitude* toward sensuality, power and comfort. These three sources of temptation are not going away. They will remain a threat to your spiritual vitality unless you maintain the right heart attitude toward them. I know none of us is a political king like David; nor do any of us live in a theocracy. Indeed, three thousand years and huge cultural differences separate us from David. But what remains the same is the heart. Because your heart's attitude toward personal freedom will critically shape your little kingdom, don't underestimate, as David did, the relentless pull of sin upon it.

Two questions frame our examination of this story. What can you learn from David's heart attitude, particularly at the time of his great sin with Bathsheba? What heart attitude led David past his sin?

What do we learn about David's heart attitude?

Let's explore two symptoms and then the precise diagnosis.

First symptom: self-centeredness. The story begins, *"Then it happened in the spring, at the time when kings go out to battle...but David stayed at Jerusalem."* Is it obvious to you that the text clearly implies that David should have gone out to battle? Of course! He is a king! Kings go to battle in the spring, presumably because the winter rains have passed and, with the harvest far off, men are available to go fight. But David stayed in Jerusalem, apparently thinking, "Let someone else do the job. I'm king, and I can set my own agenda."

Now, you and I have said that. Let someone else do the dirty work, serve in the nursery, teach the wild ones in Sunday school. Let someone else give sacrificially to the building program. Why would we think that way? Perhaps we think we're above certain menial tasks. If the toilet needs cleaning, we'll be last to volunteer. Perhaps because we crave comfort or pleasure. We might know the right thing to do, but we answer to the strongest pull on our hearts at any given moment. Perhaps it's because we anticipate failure, and we don't care to look bad. We look only to ourselves to accomplish something, surmise that we don't have what it takes, and play it safe. In such a world, we have no need to trust God.

I don't know what David was thinking, and apparently, that's not important. But it is clear what we forfeit when we think this way. When David stayed home, he missed where God was at work. When God puts you on assignment, He'll show up to display His goodness and power. Over and over again God tells Israel, "Don't go to battle without Me, or it won't be pretty!" It is always exhilarating to be used by God where He is working. But God wasn't working His righteous purposes where David's flesh worked overtime! He stayed on easy street. Can't we confess to each other that we like easy street? Our culture affords most of us an incredible easy street. Much of that is God's good gift (*"Thou dost open Thy hand, and dost satisfy the desire of every living thing."* Ps. 145:16); but what's good is often dangerous. God says He gives wealth to people; He also says wealth is very dangerous. The danger with easy street, you ask? The longer you stay on it the less inclined you are to leave it. Put another way, the more you give yourself to something, the stronger that thing will enslave you. 2 Peter 2:19 confirms, *"For by what a man is overcome, to that he is enslaved."* Eph. 4:19 echoes, *"they, having become calloused, have given themselves over to sensuality for the practice of every kind of impurity with a continual lust for more…"*

Sin never says enough. Pictured in Prov. 30:16, *"there are three things that will not be satisfied, four which never say enough…"* Sin is a taskmaster that never relents. (Romans 6:19)

But if comfort (personal peace and prosperity) is your main thing, God probably isn't working there, and your spiritual gifts aren't needed. David stayed where his gifts were not used. He was a warrior, and his gifts were required in battle! What gifts has God given you for the extension of His kingdom on the earth? I fear we think there is a spiritual gift called spectator. It fits neatly with the American spirit of individualism. David stayed home. Do you feel the underlying attitude, "I have the right, I'm in control. If I have the power to do something, it must be my prerogative to do it."

Second symptom: unguardedness. Verse 2 pictures David walking around on the roof with his close friends, his accountability partners. Right? Not quite. He is alone, in more ways than one. Yes, David is physically alone, which isn't perilous in and of itself. But with no spiritual guard in place, it is potentially devastating. How do we know his spiritual guard is down? By that upon which he gazes. He looked from his rooftop and noticed Bathsheba, apparently bathing without much to cover her beautiful body. David can't be faulted for noticing; but continuing to gaze after a glance conceived lust. *"But each one is tempted when he is carried away and enticed by his own lust. Then when lust has conceived, it gives birth to sin; and when sin is accomplished, it brings forth death."* (James 1:14-15)

Contrast this episode with Joseph's encounter with Potiphar's wife in Genesis 39:11f. Repeatedly she attempted to seduce Joseph. Finally, one time she managed to grab Joseph's garment in an attempt to seduce him, yet he fled so fast from her presence that the garment stayed in her hand! Joseph fled as fast as he could. Why? He gazed continually upon the Lord, he feared the Lord, he breathed mercy. His response centered on God. *"How then could I do this great evil and sin against God?"* (Gen. 39:9) Where on Jerusalem's rooftop is the fear of the Lord? Where is that keen sense of sin and evil David possessed while writing Psalm 139: *"O that Thou wouldst slay the wicked, O God; depart from me, therefore, men of bloodshed...Do I not loathe those who rise up against thee?"* Those very words could have been used by anyone in Bathsheba's family against David! David should have hated his own sin! David is alone physically and spiritually. He is distant from the intimacy he expounds in Psalm 139 with respect to God. Without that sense of the nearness of God, he naturally doesn't long for God's glory, a spiritual reality that is incompatible with sinful gazing.

But what of David's gazing? We see lust—he obviously craved her beauty. We see coveting—he demanded Bathsheba be his own possession. We see arrogance—he'll take what he knows is not his at any cost! Can you hear the lies? This will make me happy! What I already possess isn't enough! Just a little more! God makes exceptions for me! L'Oréal, and I'm worth it! Sin will have a man alone, but, sin never stays in isolation; it always breeds more sin. These transgressions multiply: eventually David murders her husband in a cover-up. Unrepentant sin hardens the heart, evidenced in self-deception: he proceeds merrily along until boldly confronted. *"He who conceals his sin will not prosper...he who hardens his heart will fall into calamity."* (Prov. 28:13-14)

Back to the rooftop at the moment of temptation—we don't see David's concern for holiness, being blamelessness or the Lord's reputation...in short what David *did* see when he wrote so many of the Psalms. Psalm 5:4-7 for instance says, *"For Thou art not a God who takes pleasure in wickedness; no evil dwells with Thee. The boastful shall not stand before Thine eyes; Thou dost hate all who do iniquity. Thou dost destroy those who speak falsehood; the Lord abhors the man of bloodshed and deceit. But as for me, by Thine abundant lovingkindness I will enter Thy house; at Thy temple I will bow in reverence for Thee."* Where's that in his attitude? Where is David's sense of the Lord's love and kindness?

Those symptoms, and here is the diagnosis, are simply the fruit of David's deepest sin: unbelief. Doesn't he look like some guy on a soap opera? I don't ever watch them (except a quick glance in the smoky waiting area at the gas station), but there aren't many guys passionate for holiness on those shows, are there? All of David's adultery, murder, lying, denials...this was the fruit of unbelief. I don't mean failing to believe God exists; David never questions that! Rather, unbelief is an attitude. "I know best how to make myself happy, how to rule my little kingdom. God's love isn't enough." That's the greatest threat to David: moving God temporarily to the periphery of his "worldview" while giving in to his passion for pleasure, autonomy and power. Do you believe that's also your greatest threat—underestimating the power of your cravings upon your heart? Is sex your servant? Is food your servant? Is money your servant or your master? Only when these gifts are used within the confines of God's parameters are you free.

Let me prove, from the storyline in 2 Samuel, that the attitude that led David into sin was a temporary moment of insane distrust in the goodness of God. For a season, David lived in denial of the heinousness of his actions (David reflects on this period autobiographically in Psalm 32). It took the word of God from Nathan the prophet to awaken him from his self-deceived stupor. Nathan rebuked David for all this, saying, *"Thus saith the Lord, 'I gave you everything you have, and if that wasn't enough, I would have added to you* many more things like these!'"* Not only was this a case of distrusting the goodness of God (which David gloriously articulates in Psalm 145), but in 2 Sam. 12:10, God says of David's actions, *"You despised me!"* When David was loving Bathsheba (if it feels good do it), he was hating God. James 4:4 warns, *"You adulteresses, do you not know that friendship with the world is hostility toward God? Therefore whoever wishes to be a friend of the world makes himself an enemy of God."*

Here is what you must believe: Your little kingdom may be secure "physically," but if it is centered on self, it is not safe spiritually. Ultimately, only a heart centered on the gospel is safe; you believe His love is sweeter than wine and that His grace makes the heart gladder than an abundant harvest. This is the grace that ushered you into the kingdom of Christ and that will see you safely through to the end. Every day, put your grace guard up; remind yourself of Christ's extravagant love for you! It's presence in your heart will keep indwelling sin in check, and will render external temptations less powerful. This leads to a concluding question.

What heart attitude led David past this great sin?

This is an important question because we will fail, again and again. The question really is, "How do sinners continue in joyful service, despite their failures?" Did David say, "I must try harder?" Did he turn to resolving never to sin again? Not as a foundation for his repentance. Simply determining to be better at the rules won't work. Remember, the rules had no power to restrain David the first time! On the rooftop that night, David knew the seventh commandment: *"You shall not commit adultery."* He knew the tenth commandment: *"You shall not covet."* When he ordered Uriah's death, no doubt he could have quoted to you the sixth commandment: *"You shall not murder."* David knew the Ten Commandments as well as anyone in the world! As King of Israel, he was chief custodian of the law of God. He wrote Psalm 19:7-10. *"The law of the Lord is perfect, restoring the soul; the testimony of the Lord is sure, making wise the simple. The precepts of the Lord are right, rejoicing the heart. The commandment of the Lord is pure, enlightening the eyes...They are more desirable than gold, yes, than much fine gold, Sweeter also than honey..."* Mark this well: the law has no power to restrain the flesh! Only the Holy Spirit can! Paul explicitly says that in Col. 2:23. *"...Self-abasement and severe treatment of the body...are of no value against fleshly indulgence."* Yet, *"if by the Spirit you are putting to death the deeds of the flesh, you will live."* (Rom. 8:13) What was the first step in his repentance? David went and received grace! Why? Because David was, despite this terrible fall into sin, a man after God's heart. The same grace that restored a broken David is the same grace that would sustain him, and us, until the end of our days. This is captured in Psalm 32:1-2. The only power on earth strong enough to restrain sin is the love of God. Jesus told Paul, in the context of his thorn in the flesh, whatever that was, *"My grace is sufficient for you, power is perfected in weakness."* (2 Cor. 12:9) So Paul proclaimed, *"I am what I am, by the grace of God."* (1 Cor. 15:10) This is the sure safeguard for self-deceptive hearts: living by and reveling in Christ's abundant grace. Another word for living by grace is faith. Faith is the human receptor of all the goodness Christ lavishes upon you, despite your sense of unworthiness.

Faith believes, because God says so, that *"where sin increased, grace abounded all the more."* (Romans 5:20)

"There is no faith except where we dare with tranquil hearts to stand in God's sight. This boldness arises out of a sure confidence in divine benevolence and salvation. We make promises of mercy ours by inwardly embracing them...Hence at last is born that confidence Paul calls 'peace' (Rom. 5:1)." (John Calvin, p. 561, Institutes, Book iii, Chapter ii.)

Are you afraid of grace? Actually, some people fear that if you tell them God's grace is greater than our sin it might lead to further lawlessness. They're wrong. Sure, all of us abuse grace. But it's not the fault of grace. Grace truly understood produces in us the kind of obedience God is most delighted to see. Because He is so extravagant, at great cost to Himself, we delight to serve Him. I believe this truth is evident in the postscript to the story. After the baby born to Bathsheba dies, 2 Samuel 12:29 explains that Joab asks David to come help with the battle in Rabbah. That's where the story began, Joab besieged Rabbah ... but David stayed home. This time David goes to battle, fights against and captures the whole city. God gave him a second chance. God's grace is greater than your sin. The devil would have you believe that once you blow it, you're finished—single elimination. It happened to the devil, it will not happen to you. *"Where sin abounds, grace abounds all the more."* (Rom. 5:20)

We look at this and find a paradox. You're not indispensable. God can get things done without you. Don't take yourself too *seriously, but,* on the other hand, don't fail to take yourself *soberly.* You have been given gifts for God's kingdom. Use them for His glory! There will be a day of accounting. *"For we must all appear before the judgment seat of Christ, that each one may be recompensed for his deeds in the body, whether good or bad."* (2 Cor. 5:10). Younger believers are blessed to be at an age where they only have a few regrets. As people get older and fail to do what God designed them to do, they live with serious regrets. Start asking yourself the hard question. "Is everything in my life aimed at God's glory?"

36Simon Peter said to Him, "Lord, where are you going?" Jesus answered, "Where I go, you cannot follow Me now; but you shall follow Me later." 37Peter said to Him, "Lord, why can I not follow you right now? I will lay down my life for You." 38Jesus answered, "Will you lay down your life for Me? Truly, truly, I say to you, a cock shall not crow, until you deny Me three times."

John 13:36-38

A Case Study: Overestimating the Heart

"You're not as strong as you think you are."

I rarely missed my oldest son's high school baseball games. But one time the umpires did, and the game was cancelled. The other team went home, leaving my son's team warmed up and ready to play. So his coach decided to use the opportunity for an intra-squad scrimmage. He began to look around for help with some live pitching. Guess who volunteered? Yours truly! When was the last time I pitched competitively? In the fourth grade, from about half the real distance! But I'd watched my son pitch a lot, so I was sure I could do it…

Someone threw me a glove, I went to the mound, and looked toward home plate; I couldn't believe how far the catcher was from me! Did he set up close enough to the plate? Yes! My first five warm up pitches hit the dirt in front of the plate. So I moved off the mound about six feet and pitched from there! I wasn't as strong as I thought!

Doesn't that truism translate even more noticeably and urgently in our spiritual lives? That is exactly what Jesus is purposing to show Peter (and us), "You're not as strong as you think you are."

Now we cannot for a moment question Peter's good intentions; no doubt, he is at this point profoundly devoted and sincere: *Why can't I follow you right now?* Peter loves Jesus; he wants to stick with Jesus. When he says, *"I will lay down my life for you,"* he means it most earnestly. Granted, Peter doesn't quite understand what Jesus means in John 13:33 when He says, *"you cannot come where I am going,"* but he comprehends enough that he says he is willing to be martyred. *"Even if I must die with you, I will not deny you…"* (Matthew's account, 26:34) *"He kept insisting, even if I have to die with you…"* (Mark 14:30 paraphrase) *"I am ready to go both to prison and death…"* (Luke's account, 22:33) The point is, he *thinks* he is ready, but only because Peter is self-deceived. You can be sincere, but also be sincerely self-deceived. He is not as strong as he thinks he is.

It would have been much more accurate to say, *"I can do all things through Christ who strengthens me."* (Phil. 4:13) *"I am weak, but you are strong."* (2 Cor. 12:10) *"I am what I am by the grace of God."* (1 Cor. 15:10) I'm not as strong as I think I am, *but* God is stronger than I think He is! D.A. Carson puts it well, "Peter's good intentions and self-confidence vastly outstrip his strength." Our strengths inevitably fail us and deceive us because they imply that we don't need grace.

Jesus responds to Peter's self-confidence in John 13:38. *"You will deny Me."* Notice that He makes it unmistakably specific and embarrassingly clear, *"three times before the cock crows."* Jesus leaves no room here for fudging or interpretation. We know the rest of the story—it happened exactly this way. Yes, Jesus utters a sober, somewhat rebuking prophecy to be literally fulfilled in a few hours. But isn't there more to Jesus' prophecy? Isn't the question, *"Will you lay your life down for Me"* really intended as a probe of Peter's heart? Jesus is trying to show Peter, "You really have no ability *not* to deny Me." But Peter doesn't see it. Why not? He is self-deceived; he thinks he is stronger than he really is. The Bible teaches the self-deceiving nature of sin over and over again.

It is graphically stated in Proverbs. *"There is a way which seems right to a man, but its end is the way of death."* (Prov. 14:12) *"The way of a fool is right in his own eyes."* (Prov. 12:15) *"All the ways of a man are clean in his own sight, but the Lord weighs the motives."* (Prov. 16:2) *"There is a kind of man who is pure in his own eyes, yet is not washed from his filthiness."* (Prov. 30:12) The net effect of self-deception is: I hide my weaknesses from myself; I think I'm stronger than I really am; and I don't admit how strong God is or how much I need Him. You are overestimating your strength! Peter has no response to Jesus.

Please notice that it is the word of Christ, the word of God, which cuts to the quick. This side of the cross, and the outpouring of the Holy Spirit, we can have great confidence that Jesus will also expose our self-deception. How? The same way He did with Peter—through the piercing power of the word of God. *"For the word of God is living and active and sharper than any two-edged sword, and piercing as far as the division of soul and spirit, of both joints and marrow, and able to judge the thoughts and intentions of the heart."* (Heb. 4:12)

In fact, beloved, the only reality able to plumb the depths of the human heart, piercing through the crusty layers of self-deception, is the word of God. One PCA pastor put it well:

"God's word penetrates to the bottom of our defenses, deceptions, our self-made reality. It assesses our thoughts and intentions to show us whether they are believing or unbelieving ones. God's word reveals to us whether we trust the promises of God or not. That is what I need help with in my life. I am desperate for that. The word of God penetrates to the bottom of our lives ripping the pleasant mask off the ugly face of sin. What a painful, and yet very gracious thing. What an incentive to fight for faith in God and the promises of His word. The only reason anybody sins is because at some level, he or she is deceived. They start believing the lies of sin instead of the precious promises of the word of God." (Andy Silman, Covenant Seminary Magazine, Oct./Nov. 2000)

You are not as strong as you think you are, *but* God is more gracious than you think He is. Bring your weaknesses to Christ; bring Him your heart. He will give you grace.

Do you see the grace of the John 13 passage? First, Jesus tells Peter, "You will deny Me—you're not as strong as you think you are—but I'm stronger than you think I am. I am going to love you on the heels of your shame and guilt." Jesus does not in any way minimize the heinousness of Peter's betrayal; but He says I am going to seek you and restore you in spite of it! Second, Jesus goes right from this discouraging prediction (actually meant for all of the disciples, because they all refused to believe they would deny the Lord) to words of comfort: *"Do not let your hearts be troubled."*

61

(John 14:1) Jesus specifies His intention to come again for them, to bring them to the very special place He is preparing for their eternal enjoyment. *"That where I am, you may be also."* Because I want you there, I will get you there. Jesus exhorts us to measure all that we presently have by our future hope.

What grace! A perfect heaven with Jesus ... for those whose hearts are deceived! It is such a wonderful place. Paul says it is beyond anything we've experienced: *"Things which eye has not seen and ear has not heard, and which have not entered the heart of man, all that God has prepared for those who love Him."* (1 Cor. 2:9)

What is the place Jesus will eventually go, but the place Peter cannot go? The cross. Peter cannot go there with Jesus, only Jesus can pay for his sins, only Jesus is his righteous substitute. Yes, Peter would eventually lay his life down for Jesus; he would be martyred for Christ's sake in years to come. But Peter first has to see that Jesus says, "I have to lay my life down for you." You cannot follow Me now because in order for you to enter that prepared place, you need the perfect cleansing only I can accomplish.

The hymn reminds us, "Grace, grace, God's grace, grace which is greater than all my sin." The end of the story, of course, is that Jesus restores Peter, fills him with the Holy Spirit and uses him mightily. God will use you too. But like Peter, you first must learn some important lessons. You are not as strong as you think you are. God is more gracious than you ever imagined. God will use sinners, but He will have to deal with us individually in the process. We all tend to fall off the horse in one of two directions: we are either overly self-confident, or we are faithless. We are either brash or bashful, boastful or unbelieving.

Both errors are rooted in excessive self-focus. The one, "I can do it!" The other, "God can't use me—no way!" Both errors are fruits of pride. Peter would later write in his first epistle, *"Humble yourselves under the mighty hand of God, and He will exalt you at the proper time."* (1 Peter 5:6)

Under that mighty hand, we see ourselves as we are, completely dependent on the Lord; there we serve with freedom and power, without lowering the standard. When I pitched at my son's high school, I really changed the standard by moving closer to home plate. That's our temptation in the pursuit of holiness: somehow, to lower the standards to achievable levels so we can feel good about ourselves. Grace enables us to love holiness, for it makes us more like God. Peter wrote years later, as a transformed man, *"Be holy, for God is holy"* (1 Peter 1:16), because he experienced the power of grace.

> Thou lovely source of true delight,
> Whom I unseen adore
> Unveil Thy beauties to my sight,
> That I might love Thee more,
> Oh that I might love Thee more.

> Anne Steele

[1]My son, do not forget my law, but let your heart keep my commandments; [2]for length of days and peace they will add to you. [3]Let not kindness and truth leave you; bind them around your neck; write them on the tablet of your heart.

Proverbs 3:1-3

Writing on the Heart

"Don't believe everything you tell yourself."

As we conclude Part I, we return to a concept mentioned in the first chapter, *writing on the heart.* Proverbs tells us that the wise man learns to write on his heart. The preceding chapters have sought to explain various dimensions of the heart upon which we're called to write. Now, we need to explore why and how we write on the heart.

Do you like Post-it notes as much as I do? My wife uses them to help me remember to do things. For example, it isn't enough just to send me to Sam's Club to get what we need. If I didn't have a shopping list on a Post-it, I'd walk into Sam's and forget what to buy—except what really interests *me*!

God has to do the same for us. He knows we're forgetful. You might not forget about chores, items to buy or phone calls to return. But you are forgetful *spiritually*. How do I know? God warns you specifically about forgetfulness in this passage. Proverbs tells you that God wants you to find and stay on the *path of life*. That's the main image in Proverbs for spiritual vitality, walking in fellowship with God, the good life, the pleasant way. It all begins with the *fear of the Lord*.

The fear (or reverence, awe) of the Lord begins, on the one hand, by confessing the stark truth that we never find the path of life on our own. We're asleep at the wheel, spiritually. It's not that there are no Post-its for our heart to read. There are, but they're saying the wrong thing: "Trust yourself; lean on your own understanding; only you can decide what makes you happy."

We are all born committed to find happiness independently of God, on our own terms. We are tenaciously autonomous creatures (being a law unto ourselves). The only problem with that, says God, is it will kill us: *"There is a way which seems right to a man, but in the end it is the way of death."* (Prov. 14:12) The *fear of the Lord* requires you to admit that truth, on the one hand, and on the other, *"to trust in the Lord with all your heart."* This dual aspect of the *fear of the Lord* is summed up in one of the most popular verses in the Bible. *"Trust in the Lord with all your heart, do not lean on your own understanding, in all your ways acknowledge him, and he will make your paths straight."* (Prov. 3:5)

Trust in the Lord... what does that mean? It involves taking God at His word; much like a child trusts the word of his parents, just because they are his parents. Because we trust Him, we want to know what He says and what pleases Him. That's easy to say, but how do we do it? By writing on our hearts. *"Do not let kindness and truth leave you; bind them around your neck,* write *them on the tablet of your heart* (Prov. 3:3)...*Keep my commandments and live, and my teaching as the apple of the eye. Bind them on your fingers;* write *them on the tablet of your heart."* (Prov. 7:2-3)

Why should you write on your heart?

The image of *writing on the heart* is a synonymous parallelism to the image of *binding them around your neck.* The neck connects the head and the heart; as such, what is adorned there is close to you, will guide you and speak to you—obviously, much more so than something taped to your back!

The image of heart writing focuses on two basic concepts: affections and authority. Affections are what you treasure, what you are passionate for, what you demand in order to feel whole. That thing, if you don't have it, makes you feel like dying.

Authority represents what rules you, the standards you follow, the person or thing to whom you answer. Everyone's heart is motivated by some treasure or passion. Everyone's heart is ruled by some standard. (Even those who maintain that there are no moral absolutes are ruled by that absolute!) Notice how Proverbs 7:3 brings together the heart and standards. *"My son, keep my* words *and treasure up my* commandments *with you; keep my* commandments *and live; keep* my teaching *as the apple of your eye; bind them on your fingers; write them on the tablet of your heart."*

Why is that so important to God? We naturally live by impressions, feelings, opinions, traditions, "conventional wisdom" or, perhaps, peer values. All of these inevitably fail us. Unless God changes our heart, our default mode is to lean on self-trust. "Well I've always thought of that this way…." If you want true spiritual vitality, don't believe everything you tell yourself! The *only* thing worth believing is what God says is true. What God has revealed is what we need to write on our hearts.

Proverbs 3:3 tells you to write *"kindness and truth"* on your heart. *Kindness and truth* are Hebrew words with a range of meanings. *Kindness* includes mercy and love; *truth* includes faithfulness, sincerity, upright action. That sounds good … but is that the extent of it, just *kindness and truth*? Don't we need to write more than that on our hearts? When the author puts *kindness and truth* together, he is using a literary device called hendiadys, which means "one through two." *Kindness and truth* are a two-word summary phrase for one thing: God's self-revelation. Therefore, what does your heart most desperately need? God Himself. If God Himself is not sufficient for our hearts, *nothing* is.

How does God reveal Himself to our hearts? Through His word. The Bible tells of the sufficiency of scripture for our hearts. *"His divine power has granted to us all things that pertain to life and godliness, through the knowledge of his who called us to his own glory and excellence, by which he has granted to us his precious and very great promises…"* (2 Peter 1:3) For example, when you are discouraged and need encouragement, the Bible has the promises you need—all of them, not just a few to be supplemented with food or drink or shopping or the latest self-help book. When you're straying and need instruction or correction, the Bible has all the precepts you need—not some of them supplemented with human wisdom, but all of them. *"All scripture is inspired by God, and profitable for teaching, reproof, correction, and training in righteousness, that the man of God may be adequate, equipped for every good work."* (2 Tim. 3:16)[*]

But we must take this a step farther. If *kindness and truth* are a summary of God's character and His word, then they also must be a "one-through-two" description of Jesus, the kindness and truth of God made flesh. When John reflects on the wonder of the incarnation (John 1:14), he does so in those terms. *The word became flesh and dwelt among us, full of grace and truth.* Paul also uses the same designation for Jesus. *"But when the kindness of God our savior appeared..."* (Titus 2:14) Therefore, the command to write *kindness and truth* on your heart is fulfilled by trusting Christ and asking Him to fill your heart with His presence.

Do you see why you need Christ? The command to write *kindness and truth* on our hearts proves us lawbreakers, does it not? Don't we all suffer from serious "writer's block?" We falter, stumble and fail at faithfully writing these things on the heart! Such failure drives us to the One who can forgive us for failing to do what God requires. It compels us to trust in the One who lived perfectly in our stead. Once you've received Christ as your complete salvation before the Father, you also possess in Christ all the fullness of God's gifts of love and truth. How? Jesus gladly writes them on your heart by His Spirit, so that you might know God is for you, and so you might bless others through kindness and truth.

---

[*] All of Psalm 119 is a meditation on the sufficiency of scripture.

How do you write on the heart?

You write on your heart the same way you use a Post-it. Keep it in front of you and act on it. If I take my wife's Post-it with me to Sam's Club, it will do me no good until I look at it and I take action on it. Christians know that behavior always flows out of your beliefs; therefore, we are always seeking to become increasingly biblical thinkers. We don't see it as an option.

In Proverbs 2:4, we're exhorted to *"seek for wisdom as for silver, search for her as for hidden treasure."* That implies *intensity*: persistently refusing to give up until you find it. It also implies *reward:* you wouldn't leave it there once you found it! We don't want to merely read the Bible and leave in it all God's promises and precepts; we want to take them with us wherever we are. We want them to be our light, inflaming our affections, setting the standards for our conduct. *"Don't be hearers of the word only, but doers of it also."* (James 1:21)

Jesus prayed (John 17:17) to His Father for all His disciples: *"Sanctify them in the truth, your word is truth."* Jesus is loving, empowering, changing and fellowshipping with us through His word. The holiest and happiest believers are those who marinate their hearts continuously in God's word. *"Do not be conformed to this world, but be transformed by the renewing of your mind..."* (Rom. 12:2) *"Whatsoever things are true, honorable, just, pure, lovely, commendable, any excellence or worthy of praise, let your mind dwell on these things."* (Phil. 4:8) *"We are destroying speculations and every lofty thing raised up against the knowledge of God and we are taking every thought captive to the obedience of Christ."* (2 Cor. 10:5)

So you write on the heart by reading the Bible—slowly, meditatively, probingly. Ask questions of the text: What does the text reveal about God? My sin? The work of the Savior? Write important verses on cards and review them for memory. Discuss it with others. And, of course, put it to work, apply it. Only when you act on God's word will you find it powerful to break the stranglehold of false pleasures and counterfeit lovers over your heart.

Constant exposure to the word of God, through personal reading, and hearing it preached and taught in church, enables you constantly to examine, "Where is the breakdown in my heart-writing?" Again, think in terms of affection and authority, "Why do I do this?" What do I crave more than God? Why isn't the promise of God's love enough? What must I be writing on my heart that I think I need something other than God? What treasure am I pursuing? By whose standard am I seeking to live? As you consistently apply these questions to your life, you will find a beautiful script of holiness, joy and Christ-likeness being written on your heart. Nothing will compare to the freedom and power they produce.

Next, we examine the most amazing miracle of human existence: how faith in Christ comes to the heart.

PART II

THE HEART SET FREE

[16]For God so loved the world, that He gave His only begotten Son, that whoever believes in Him should not perish, but have eternal life. [17]For God did not send His Son into the world to judge the world; but that the world should be saved through Him. [18]He who believes in Him is not judged; he who does not believe has been judged already, because he has not believed in the name of the only begotten Son of God. [19]And this is the judgment, that the light is come into the world, and men loved the darkness rather than the light; for their deeds were evil. [20]For everyone who does evil hates the light, and does not come to the light, lest his deeds should be exposed. [21]But he who practices the truth comes to the light, that his deeds may be manifested as having been wrought in God.

John 3:16-21

Believing with the Heart

"The heart always acts according to its desires."

Here's a pretty easy question: What is the most publicized scripture verse in America? Everyone has seen John 3:16 somewhere on the landscape and your best bet is either on a bumper sticker or at a sporting event, usually in the end zone! Most Christians know John 3:16, probably the majority has it memorized. And that's great; it is a tremendous verse encapsulating the gospel. But how many Christians understand *the doctrine* that John 3:16 teaches, both explicitly and implicitly? Probably not nearly enough! As popular as this verse is, John 3:16 is often misapplied doctrinally. What's the problem with that? Misapplied doctrines don't help you; they can hurt you. They are like a bad front-end alignment on your car. You may be able to get by for a while, but sooner or later, you are going to have problems.

This text centers on the human activity *believing*. It mentions this two times in verses 16-17. With what is believing directly contrasted? *Not believing,* highlighted two times in verse 18. What are we told specifically to believe? *Believe in Christ.* So we could call this the *Doctrine of Believing*, or perhaps *the Doctrine of Saving Faith*, since the text is clearly concerned with the *"world being saved through Him."* (v. 17) I like to see this passage as painting a landscape of belief. John's stated purpose for revealing to us the glory of Jesus Christ is that we might believe. *"But these have been written that you may believe that Jesus is the Christ, the Son of God; and that believing you may have life in His name."* (John 20:31)

The doctrine of believing involves all sorts of interesting questions. Let's try, however, to restrict our questions to those that principally rise directly out of the text. *Why doesn't* everyone *believe the gospel? Why does* anyone *believe the gospel?* That's really two sides of the same coin—*the belief coin.* And aren't these issues we wonder about? Why hasn't Uncle Joe become a Christian? Why am I a Christian and not my father? Am I sure I am a Christian? These are practical, pressing questions, which beg us for doctrinal clarity.

Why doesn't everyone believe the gospel?

This question presupposes a more fundamental issue. Why do people believe what they believe, and do what they do? The biblical answer is *because of their desires.* We always act out of what we believe or desire at any given moment. This is the sense in which human beings have *free will.* God isn't coercing us to do anything; He certainly isn't actively creating sinful desires or unbelief in anyone's heart. The best term for this is *free human agency.* We are, in God's sight, morally responsible beings who have the ability to choose certain things. We have the freedom to choose one thing or another, but the ability to choose only what we want. We are not robots or puppets. We always act out of our own inclinations, unforced by outside powers.

Yet having said that, we must immediately stress that the Bible also teaches an apparently contradictory truth, that is, God is absolutely sovereign over the affairs of man. Nothing happens without His permission; *He works all things after the counsel of his own will.* (Eph. 1:11) God knows the future because He predestines it. He neither learns nor forgets. Is this hard to understand? Yes! Do you have to understand this mystery completely to go to heaven? No! But does the Bible clearly teach this tension? Unapologetically! Look at Acts 2:23 for a perfect rendering of this tension. *"This Jesus, delivered up by the predetermined plan and foreknowledge of God, you nailed to a cross by the hands of godless men and put him to death..."* This truth is echoed in the prayer of Acts 4:27-28. *"For truly in this city there were gathered together against Thy holy servant Jesus...to do whatever Thy hand and Thy purpose predestined to occur."* Do you see the amazing tension assumed in these two verses? God was utterly sovereign over the event of Jesus' death, yet those who perpetrated it were completely responsible. Both God's sovereignty *and* human responsibility are asserted, though from a human point of view we may wonder how it could be so.

Let's go back to the issue at hand. The million-dollar question really becomes, *"Who has a desire for God?"* Does man as he is born naturally have any desire for the Lord or the things of the Lord? There's no point talking about free will, since we never *will* what we don't desire (or, put positively, we *will* only what we desire). Who naturally has an internal, already existing desire to please God, pursue God or know God? No one! We're all stillborn spiritually. Just as a physically dead person has no appetite for food, so a spiritually dead person has no appetite for God. This is what the Bible calls *spiritual death.* Eph. 2:1 says, *"And you were* dead *in your trespasses and sins..."*

Rom. 3:13ff: *"There is none righteous, no not one; there is none who understands, there is none who seeks for God, all have turned aside..."* John 1:5 teaches the same truth: *"And the light shines in the darkness, and the darkness did not comprehend it."* We're all blind, dull, deaf; we just don't get it spiritually. *"But a natural man does not accept the things of the Spirit; for they are foolishness to him, and he cannot understand them, because they are spiritually appraised."* (1 Cor. 2:14) In our heart of hearts, we want to have nothing to do with God. Rarely does an unbeliever admit this; but it is so, nonetheless. Do you feel the gravity of the indictment of Proverbs 19:4, *"The foolishness of man subverts his way, and his heart* rages *against the Lord"* and 14:2, *"He who walks uprightly fears the Lord, but he who is crooked in his ways* despises *Him?"*

The same truth is expressed here in the text in John 3:19, *"...the light has come into the world, and men loved the darkness rather than the light."* The point, beloved, is that no one can believe until he is given the desire to believe. That was one of Jesus' points to Nicodemus: *unless you are born from above, you cannot see the kingdom.* (John 3:3 paraphrase) The Holy Spirit must first breathe life into your dead heart, thus creating a desire for God that never existed. *"For just as the Father raises the dead and gives them life, even so the Son also gives life to whom He wishes."* (John 5:21)

So the question, why doesn't everyone believe the gospel, is most accurately answered, *they can't (or won't) believe because they have no desire to believe.* Many of us have seen this in our experience of sharing the love of Christ. It seems like the good news goes in one ear and out the other. You realize you are asking someone for a commitment to Christ, yet he or she is restrained by a prior commitment to something else. The unbeliever's prior commitment is, according to John 3:19, *to the darkness.* Even though the light of God's glory shines constantly, and the witness of Christ has come to many parts of the world, people would rather grope in the pitch-black cave of unbelief, searching for tiny gems of happiness, than look to the spotlight of the Savior to lead them to safety.

Do you see the insanity of sin? *We desire the darkness.* Darkness is life without God, an existence independent of God, characterized by this attitude, *"There is a way which seems right to a man, but its end is the way of death."* (Proverbs 14:12) It's not as though we are innocently waiting for the light. Unbelief is tenaciously motivated by hatred of the light, love of evil and fear of being exposed. (John 3:20) Each of these could be explored in detail, but not now for our present purposes.

What doctrine is this we're uncovering? *The Depravity of Man.* Sin has tainted every part of his constitution, and most tragically, his desires. All I desire is self-gratification—sin. I have no appetite for God. That's why John 3:18 can declare that *we are already judged.* Because we are *by nature children of wrath* (Eph. 2:3), we're born under judgment, that is, *the wrath of God abides on us.* (John 3:36).

Why does anyone believe the gospel?

Ultimately, it is because they want to believe it. Every person that becomes a Christian does so because he or she wants to. We may wrestle, question, and resist for a season, but when we finally repent and believe, we do so willingly. But, if no one is born with the desire, where then did it come from? Do you have it because you were born to Christian parents? No, John already explained in 1:13 that, *"you were not born of blood, nor of the will of the flesh, nor of the will of man, but of God."* Who changed your desires? The Holy Spirit (John 1:13; 3:3) *"No one can come to Me, unless the Father who sent Me draws him."* (John 6:44)

Notice that this verse expresses ability, not permission. The same idea is present in Deuteronomy 29:4, *"Yet to this day the Lord has not given you a heart to know, nor eyes to see, nor ears to hear."*

If anyone has the heart to know or eyes to see or ears to hear, it is because God gave it. Hear Jesus' plain articulation of this in Matt. 11:27. *"All things have been handed over to Me by My Father; and no one knows the Son, except the Father; nor does anyone know the Father, except the Son, and anyone to whom* the Son wills to reveal Him.*"* Lydia, in Acts 16:14, illustrates this. *"The Lord opened her heart to understand the things spoken by Paul."*

This is the doctrine called *Irresistible Grace.* Does sinful man resist God's kindness? Constantly. But, when God sets His love upon us to save us by the regenerating power of the Spirit, no one can resist that. And who would want to? So in the nature of the case, regeneration (being born again by the Spirit) always precedes faith (believing the promise of the gospel at conversion). *"Even when we were dead in our transgressions, He made us alive together with Christ..."* (Ephesians 2:4) *"...He caused you to be born again..."* (1 Peter 1:3) *"In the exercise of His will He brought us forth by the word of truth..."* (James 1:18)

Now you may be making some mental connections and wondering, does that mean God chooses some to have the eyes of faith and not others? Evidently. Jesus said in John 15:16, *"you did not choose me, but I chose you."* *"Jacob I loved, but Esau I hated...I will have mercy on who I will have mercy, and I will have compassion on whom I will have compassion...So then it* [salvation] *does not depend on the man who wills or the man who runs, but on God who has mercy."* (Romans 9:13-16) In this context, we are able to make sense out of verses like, *"The Lord has made everything for its own purpose, even the wicked for the day of judgment."* (Prov. 16:4) *"...For they stumble because they are disobedient to the word, and to this doom they were also appointed."* (1 Peter 2:8)

We call this the doctrine of *Unconditional Election;* God saves people based solely on His own pleasure, not based on anything in them or God foreseeing anything they would do. Sadly, this is a hard doctrine for most Americans to get their hearts around. I believe there is a fairly strong "I elect God" spirit in America. But you have to agree, if everything we have seen thus far is true, unconditional election is the only way anyone could possibly be saved.

Why do we quarrel with God if, for His own pleasure and glory He changes the desire of some rebels, and gives other rebels what they want? This is not an issue of justice, is it? Some will, regretfully, get justice—the very thing they deserve. Others will, *to the praise of His glorious grace* (Eph. 1:6), receive mercy. *All* who desire to be saved *will be* saved! There really isn't any mystery there; Eph. 1:4 clearly states *that God chose us in Christ before the foundation of the world.* The mystery is ... why does anyone receive mercy? God is only obligated to deal out retribution. Why does anyone believe?

The question for you today is, "Why would you now refuse His mercy, having just heard about it?" Only because you want to refuse it. It is not difficult to understand: You deserve to die for your sins, but God gave His Son Jesus to die in the place of any who believe in Him. That's the gracious offer of John 3:16, *"whoever believes has eternal life."* As far as you are concerned, God freely offers you eternal life in His Son. Take it! He is commanding you to believe! He is commanding you to compare eternal life with eternal perishing! The Father, out of His great love, sent the Son to save us from perishing. Jesus has come this first time around to save (John 3:17), indicating that the next time He comes He'll judge with absolute finality. There will be no second chances. *"It is appointed for all men to die once, and after this comes judgment."* (Hebrews 9:27) Today is the day to be saved through Christ. (2 Cor. 6:2)

This is the doctrine we call the *Free Offer of the Gospel. Anyone hearing the message can be saved.* It's for the world, not just the Jews. Nicodemus would have embraced the typical Pharisee's view that the Messiah was coming to establish the Jewish nation, and to destroy the Gentiles. But the stress of the free offer of the gospel is that the cross can save anyone, Jew or Gentile. *"God so loved the world..."* Salvation isn't restricted to the smart, the wealthy, any race, any nationality. It's for anyone! Are you an "anyone?" Then you can be saved! *"...Whoever believes shall not perish but have eternal life..."* (John 3:16) "Whoever *calls on the name of the Lord shall be saved!"* (Romans 10:13) *"God is now declaring to men that* all everywhere *should repent..."* (Acts 17:30)

But you may protest: *I don't have the desire*! Of course, we understand—the Bible says you won't! But you must ask for it. *But I am unwilling*! Right! Thanks for being honest, the Bible says as much about all of us! *But,* you must ask to be willing, and repent of your steadfast refusal to bow before the Lord who made you!

Some object at this point with the oft-heard question: But what about the innocent native in Africa? First, he or she is not innocent; we've already established that. God will deal justly with them. Paul explains in Romans 1 that everyone knows God—God making Himself evident in the creation—yet all refuse to acknowledge Him and exchange the truth of God for a lie. (Romans 1:19f) Second, don't let someone else's ignorance be a cause of your refusal to deal honestly with the knowledge you have!

So how do you begin to feel the desire? By hearing the gospel. God uses the gospel to flame into fire the desire. *"Faith comes through hearing, and hearing by the word of Christ."* (Rom. 10:17) The Holy Spirit works mysteriously to create belief, but it is your belief, and it is always a believing grounded in gospel revelation. Here is a maxim: No one can believe without the gospel; everyone who believes does so because of the gospel. Do you see *it must be the Spirit who creates the desire* for salvation? He uses the gospel to create faith. Is there a mystery here? Yes. Why does God awaken people when He does? I don't know. But I do know this awakening is completely by His grace, from beginning to end.

What difference does it make if you believe these doctrines? Let me suggest several differences. You can be more playful. You can relax. God is sovereign; God saved you. You should be more thankful. You should have perished in your sins but God saved you! You should be more humble. Can you believe it? He saved a person like you! You should be more patient with others. Wouldn't you be as bad off as anyone else would but for the grace of God? You should begin to share Jesus' concern for the peril of unsaved people.

In the next chapter, we will explore how Jesus used a vivid parable to describe the way the heart receives the word of God.

³And He spoke many things to them in parables, saying, "Behold, the sower went out to sow; ⁴and as he sowed, some seeds fell beside the road, and the birds came and devoured them. ⁵And others fell upon the rocky places, where they did not have much soil; and immediately they sprang up, because they had no depth of soil. ⁶But when the sun had risen, they were scorched; and because they had no root, they withered away. ⁷And others fell among the thorns, and the thorns came up and choked them out. ⁸And others fell on the good soil, and yielded a crop, some a hundredfold, some sixty, and some thirty. ⁹He who has ears to hear, let him hear."

Matthew 13:3-9

The Heart: Soil for the Word of God

"The word of the gospel is not advice, but an announcement."[*]

Bible-believing Christians and their pastors have many things in common, not the least of which is a passion for proper interpretation of the Bible. Like the doctor who strives to correctly interpret his patient's lab results, or like the financial investor who seeks to interpret the meaning of economic indicators, Bible-believers and their pastors want nothing less than the most accurate, faithful, true interpretation of God's holy word. The history of the Church proves it is easy to misinterpret the Bible; and that makes for a very dangerous enterprise, because misinterpreted texts usually produce misapplied texts, and misapplied texts do to your soul what misapplied medicine does to your body.

That analogy I just made between medicine and Scripture is a parable—the word literally means "comparison," and in the Old Testament, the word is one of the central ideas related to "proverb." Jesus taught predominantly with stories and parables, which, by definition, need interpretation. People have to wonder, *"What did He mean by that?"* The best thing about the parable of the sower is we know the interpretation, because Jesus gives it to us! God Himself in Christ provides the correct interpretation.

Parables are stories standing for deeper truths. They are object lessons requiring reflection and thought. So Jesus said in Luke 8:18,

---

[*] Dr. Tim Keller

"Carefully consider how you listen." Translated: parables interpret you.

Parables do not reinforce conventional wisdom as much as they introduce otherwise unknown truths about the kingdom of God. Virtually all of them refer to the kingdom of God. God's kingdom is a revelation of eternal realities, which are not innately obvious to fallen creatures. Parables compare eternal realities to that which is familiar—making the unknown illumined by the known.

They are two types of parables: narrative, which have a "once upon a time" quality, and similitudes, comparisons made with a word story. Both types have universal appeal because they connect with our experience and, in one way or another, lead us to a point of crisis or decision. See if you detect in the parable in Matthew 13:3-9 a narrative, the comparing of eternal realities to what is known, and the design to lead hearers to a point of decision.

Consider the obvious. Most people in His audience (an especially huge one because many were so drawn to the notion in Jesus' teaching about the reign of God breaking in) know something about the joys and struggles of farming. The drama is easily imagined; fields aren't perfectly manicured, as they begin at the road and move out into the good soil. The focus is not on the sower but rather on the seed. The focus of the seed is on where it falls—four types of soil, and correspondingly, four types of growth. But the best aspect of this parable is that Jesus interprets it for us!

Before Jesus interprets the parable, He responds to a question from His disciples, the inner Twelve handpicked for His mission. They ask a reasonable, expected question: *why do you teach in parables?* We might have guessed that His answer would be something like this. "I'm a Jew; we think principally in terms of pictures, not like the Greeks who think in propositions. In rabbi school, they taught us to be vivid, to be interesting, and that stories are very effective means of communicating truth." That would all be true. But that's not how Jesus answers. Jesus answers in terms the Old Testament sets out. Isaiah prophesied about the people of

Jesus' day, the Jews. They will hear the message of the kingdom, but won't get it. (Matt. 13:15)

That Jesus taught in parables reveals two things. First, it was a judgment on the hardness of hearts of the Jews of His generation. The elusiveness of parables, that they didn't naturally *get it*, proves their hearts were hard. The parables functioned to crystallize opposition to Jesus that had already formed in their hearts. Second, it also proves election. None of us will ever *get* the kingdom unless God opens our eyes. Jesus taught the disciples plainly, because He called them aside. D.A. Carson summarizes, "Jesus teaches in such a way as to harden those already hard of heart and offended by the gospel, and to enlighten His disciples."

Most people respond to this notion in two ways. One, you may object and protest, "Wait a minute, I want to understand. Don't keep spiritual truth from me!" Or, two, you may humbly wonder what you must do in order to *get* the kingdom? To what kind of heart does the kingdom come? What should I ask God to do for me so I can embrace the king and His message?

Illustrative are the words of the early Church father Anselm, "Faith is seeking understanding to embrace the truth." That is exactly the question the parable answers. That's why Matthew placed it first before all the other parables. This parable reveals the key to understanding all the others. So Mark 4:13 says, *"Do you not understand this parable? And how will you understand all the parables?"*

Notice how the parable tacitly asks you not to be the sower, or the seed, but to come out in the field and watch the seed (the message of the kingdom) be scattered. Watch on what soil (heart) the seed lands, and wonder, "Is that what my heart is like?" Are you proud? "Nobody tells me what to do or believe! I'm my own person! This is America; I have a right to my own opinion." Are you fearful? "If I believe that, what will happen to me?" Stubborn? "If I believe that I'll have to stop certain things, and I can't give them up." Maybe you are humble. "God is really the only one who can help me understand."

The parable is for everyone reading it; all of us have some contact with the kingdom of God. The most critical question you could ask yourself is, "What is my heart's relationship to the message of the kingdom?" Is it advice, *"Be a good person?"* Or an announcement, *"God has accepted you?"* Is Jesus a personal trainer, or is He salvation itself?

Here is Jesus' interpretation. *"Hear then the parable of the sower. When any hears the word of the kingdom, and does not understand it, the evil one comes and snatches away what has been sown in his heart. This is the one on whom seed was sown beside the road. And the one on whom seed was sown in rocky places, this is the man who hears the word and immediately receives it with joy; yet he has no firm root in himself, but is only temporary, and when affliction or persecution arises because of the word, immediately he falls away. And the one on whom seed was sown among the thorns, this is the man who hears the word, and the worry of the world, and the deceitfulness of riches choke the word, and it becomes unfruitful. And the one on whom seed was sown on the good ground, this is the man who hears the word and understands it; who indeed bears fruit, and brings forth, some a hundred, some sixty and some thirty."* (Matt. 13:18-23) There are, according to Jesus, four types of people who have contact with the kingdom of God.

The casual: Here are folks who in one way or another are exposed to the message. Because their hearts are stony, the seed is plucked up by Satan. In Rabbinic literature, birds were symbols of the devil. He hates it when we believe the truth. He always promotes death and lies. Ultimately, it isn't the fault of the devil; it is one's hard heart, in which there's no place for truth.

The shallow: Notice that there is a good start—*"they received the word with joy."* (Matt. 13:20) But the heat of trials reveals our motives. I was in it for me, to get God to serve me. Unless our roots go deep, we'll eventually find God unattractive or unfair.

The worldly: These folks apparently begin to grow, but are deceived by wealth, pleasures and worries. Their hearts become divided. The psalmist says, *"Unite my heart to fear thy name. If I regard iniquity you won't hear."* (Ps. 86:11) This person doesn't take the ravages of indwelling sin seriously enough. He gives in to his passions. You must ask constantly, what controls me?

The responsive: The seed, the word of God, is alive, it comes in to the heart and the Spirit uses it to produce fruit. God looks upon the field of your labors for Christ and delights.

One last observation: the focus of the parable is clearly on the ground; therefore, look at your heart. But, Jesus calls it the parable of the sower. Why not call it the parable of the soils or the seed. Wouldn't those words be more accurate? I'm guessing He does so for at least two reasons. The parable *does* illustrate the ministry of Jesus' kingdom: the word of it is sown everywhere, and responses vary. Just because it doesn't take the world by storm doesn't mean it isn't true. The kingdom advances slowly. Also, the sower chooses the seed he sows. The seed is the word of the kingdom. What is that? It's the word of Christ's grace, His love, which comes to the needy. The kingdom is the intervention of God in history, starting the renewal of the cosmos, reversing the effects of the curse. God starts with people.

Are you a person with whom God is reversing the effects of sin? Your heart's reception to the word of God is sure evidence.

[10]And in Him you have been made complete, and He is the head of all rule and authority; [11]and in Him you were also circumcised with a circumcision made without hands, in the removal of the body of the flesh by the circumcision of Christ; [12]having been buried with Him in baptism, in which you were also raised up with Him through faith in the working of God, who raised Him from the dead. [13]And when you were dead in your transgressions and the uncircumcision of your flesh, He made you alive together with Him, having forgiven us all our transgressions, [14]having cancelled out the certificate of debt consisting of decrees against us and which was hostile to us; and He has taken it out of the way, having nailed it to the cross. [15]When He had disarmed the rulers and authorities, He made a public display of them, having triumphed over them through Him.

Colossians 2:10-15

A Heart Free from Condemnation

*"Your heart is more wicked than you ever dared to imagine,
but you are more loved than you ever dreamt possible."*[*]

Anyone keeping up with the evolution of military weaponry
knows that all U.S. combat troops wear helmets equipped with
night vision goggles. It's astounding to me: soldiers can see things
at night otherwise completely undetected by the naked eye.
Whether or not a soldier has them makes him either very
vulnerable to his enemy or significantly advantaged. Which word
describes you spiritually: vulnerable or advantaged? In Colossians
2:10-15, Paul is showing the Colossians how much advantage they
have spiritually, *"you've been filled with Christ who is the fullness
of God."*

False teachers, however, would have the Christians there
believe that they remain spiritually vulnerable until they embrace
certain Gnostic practices and rituals. Paul sounds an emphatic *no*!
He smells in the heretical teaching the same error he detects
everywhere the gospel is preached: God can do more for you than
He's already done in Christ. The false teachers don't acknowledge
what God has already accomplished for believers in Christ. Why
not? They don't have spiritual night-vision goggles. So in these
verses, Paul holds up spiritual night vision goggles to his readers'
eyes so that they can clearly behold the advantage they have
spiritually in the death and resurrection of Jesus Christ.

---

[*] Dr. Tim Keller

To the naked eye—the unbelieving observer—Jesus' death was just another Roman crucifixion, and His resurrection some fanciful lie or myth. But though invisible to the naked eye, once we put on spiritual night vision goggles, we who live out our lives in enemy territory, who battle constantly with sin and Satan, clearly detect the difference between safety and danger, life and death, freedom and slavery, friend and foe. We see, in other words, in the cross and empty tomb, what God has already done for us through His Son, what a decisive blow God has already dealt to our enemies. Only when you embrace the wonderful reality of Jesus' victory—through spiritual night vision goggles—will you safely negotiate enemy territory (going where the Savior leads, not Satan), confidently refuse to be duped by false teaching, and experience spiritual fullness and freedom.

To flesh out what God has already accomplished for us in Christ, Paul provides three pictures in Colossians 2 of God's work on our behalf. The whole focus in verses 11-15 is on God's work for us; God is the subject of each of the five sentences here. Verse 11, God circumcised you; verse 12, God raised you; verse 13, God made you alive by uniting you to Jesus; verse 14, God forgave you and cancelled your debt; verse 15, God triumphed by disarming your opponents.

God made you alive by uniting you to Jesus.

Paul holds up the spiritual night vision goggles and says, "I want you to see how someone becomes a Christian." Essentially, becoming a Christian is a spiritual resurrection; it is God doing inside you spiritually what He did to Jesus physically.

To help us appreciate God's power, Paul tells us what we were before coming to life spiritually: *"You were dead in your trespasses and the uncircumcision of your flesh."* (v. 13) The Gentile converts in the church would see themselves physically uncircumcised, but for Paul that is a symbol of all humanity's alienation from God. What is *"dead in trespasses* [sins]*?"* Since his readers are physically alive, it obviously means they are

88

spiritually dead. Because all of Adam's posterity inherits the guilt of his sin, all of us are born alienated from God, hostile to God. We have an aversion to God. Just as a physically dead person has no appetite for food, so a spiritually dead person has no appetite for God.

Many Christians teach that spiritual death is *separation from God.* Indeed, it is that, but more. We could be separated from God but still want Him, much like a child could be separated from his parent but remains desirous of the parent's love and protection. Spiritual death means we are separated by our own choice and we want nothing to do with God. Our basic attitude is, keep your grubby hands off of my life. We are *by nature children of wrath.* (Eph. 2:3) Once Adam and Eve sinned in the Garden of Eden, their nature, created originally by God to be righteous and holy, changed. In keeping with God's warning that *"in the day you eat of it* [the tree of the knowledge of good and evil] *you shall surely die"* (Gen. 2:17), their glorious, pristine, morally beautiful nature died; it completely ceased to be. From that point on, they and all of their posterity were enslaved to a fallen, sin-dominated nature. So David could say in Psalm 51:5, *"I was brought forth in iniquity, in sin my mother conceived me."*

Now this doesn't for a minute mean people aren't religious—they are! All human beings worship something. But because of spiritual death, our propensity is to redefine God on our own terms, to worship something created rather than the Creator. We are unwilling and unable to keep covenant or relationship with the Creator. Spiritual night vision sees this because the Holy Spirit has convicted us of sin, righteousness and judgment. He drops from our eyes these rose-colored scales through which we formerly saw ourselves as basically good, and God as basically tolerant...undesirable...unnecessary. The prophet Ezekiel saw this in a vision of a valley of dry bones, a picture of humanity dead in sin. (Ezekiel 37) Mary and Martha, friends of Jesus whose brother Lazarus died, also witnessed a living parable of spiritual resurrection when Jesus called Lazarus forth from the tomb. (John 11) These are pictures of how someone becomes a Christian. Jesus speaks forth the word of power and the Spirit creates faith in the heart to believe it. If sin kills, the Spirit makes alive. So how does God save sinners? He does it by uniting them to His Son through faith (Col. 2:12). With spiritual night vision goggles, we understand that as Jesus burst through the tomb from death, so did we. Faith unites us to Christ; what is true of Him is true of all who trust Him. When Jesus was raised, so were you, though the power of salvation wasn't applied until the time of your conversion.

Why does God do this? After all, the world is full of people who want nothing to do with God. A parallel passage in Ephesians 2:4 reveals God's motive. *"But God, being rich in mercy, because of his great love with which he loved us..."* The salvation of undeserving sinners is nothing less than the display of the glory of the riches of God's mercy and grace in Christ.

So do you see that there are only two kinds of individuals in the world, those that need faith and those that have it? Those that need it may (actually, they must!) simply ask for it. This is God's promise: *"Everyone who calls on the name of the Lord will be saved."* (Rom. 10:13) Christ will save you beloved, flee to Him now. *Whoever believes in Him will not perish but have everlasting life.* (John 3:16)

Those that have been given faith—thank Him! You now see that religion doesn't save you; philosophy doesn't save you; moral exertion can't save you. God saves you in His Son!

God forgave you and cancelled your debt.

It certainly is a very nice thing for God to have given us spiritual life when we were hopelessly helplessly dead in our sins. But that's not the whole picture. Spiritual night vision goggles see more. Sin creates a debt. Because God is our holy Creator and Sustainer, we owe God perfect obedience and worship. Therefore any failure to give God His due is cosmic treason—a slap in His face. There we sit in His lap as His created beings—God graciously giving us life and breath—slapping Him in the face saying, "Leave me alone, keep Your hands off my life." Spiritual vision can see that; it understands that when we sin we're writing an IOU to God. That's this word *"certificate of debt"*—a document on which a debt is recorded, written in one's own hand as proof of obligation. Col. 2:14 reports the bad news: *"it decrees against us."* We can't fulfill the *legal demands of the law.* Picture yourself as that lone Chinese man standing before the army tank in Tiananmen Square, and the tank being the demand of the law.

Everything God demands we fail to deliver, and, what we think we do well is tainted by pride, self-interest and a lack of passion for God's glory. Faith sees with spiritual goggles Jesus on the cross pleading, "Bring that record of debt to me. If you die with it in your hands, it will condemn you to hell." Faith looks at the Savior on the cross and trusts, "you died there for me, you'll gladly take my sin from me." This is the heart of Christianity. Helpless sinners bringing all they have to offer God—sin and their pride-tainted effort to gain God's approval—and God nails it through the flesh of His Son on the cross. *"He Himself bore our sins in His body on the tree."* (1 Peter 2:24) Jesus took the tank's artillery shell for you!

Notice the effects of God nailing our sin there. The debt is canceled or wiped out (Col. 2:14). The power of the law, its ability to render us guilty and therefore kill us, is destroyed. The tank now has neither ammunition nor motor. He *has forgiven us all our transgressions.* (2:13) God at the cross declares good news, "I accept my Son's death as sufficient to pay for your sins." Who would imagine such an exchange possible? We give Jesus our record of sin; He grants forgiveness and His perfect record. *"He made Him who knew no sin to be sin on our behalf, that we might become the righteousness of God in Him."* (2 Cor. 5:21) Some people maintain that our interpretation of the cross is cruel, that God the Father would never do that to His Son. Such is an appraisal of the cross without spiritual vision. The immense love of God for us in the death of Christ cannot be understood without spiritual night vision goggles.

Now please understand that this spiritual vision not only sees the cross differently, but everything else as well. As you first and foremost define yourself as a person coming to Christ with a record of debt, how can you turn around and be critical? How can you be prideful? How can you not be generous, thinking that God just isn't worth more than a few bucks here and there? How could you enjoy someone else's struggle? How can you receive Jesus' perfect record as a gift and still act as if you need to do more to please God? Scrutinize the trophies of your heart. Is what you cherish really of lasting value and eternal significance? If I come home from a round of golf, and happened to have played well (an unusual occurrence!), what is more important, that everyone know about this little feat, or that my family knows they are infinitely more important than a passing outing on the golf course?

God triumphed by disarming your opponents.

If you were in the middle of combat with the enemy, and advanced on their position at night, wearing your night-vision goggles, you'd be apprehensive, alert or possibly fearful. But if with your night vision goggles, you saw the enemy stripped of his weapons you'd burst with confidence—fear would turn to joy, apprehension to relief.

That's the picture in Col. 2:15. Again, to the naked eye Jesus of Nazareth expired on the cross outside Jerusalem at 3 p.m. on a Friday two thousand years ago. But with the benefit of spiritual night vision, verse 15 tells us that in the spiritual realm Jesus triumphed over the devil. Oh what great irony! The Romans and Jews thought they were triumphing over Jesus. Satan thought he had finally destroyed Jesus—having started with the decree by Herod to kill all the baby boys in Israel after Jesus' birth, tempting Jesus in the wilderness 40 days, and moving Judas' heart to betray Him. Little did he know that as Jesus breathed His last on the cross, His foot crushed the head of Satan, fulfilling the promise of Genesis 3:15, *"He [Jesus] shall bruise you [Satan] on the head and he shall bruise you on the heel."* Verse 15 says He *disarmed the rulers and authorities.* He snatched the accusing sword from

Satan and publicly shamed him, not behind the veil in the temple but for all the world to see.

The word *triumph* refers to the Roman victory procession after a foreign battle. The conquering general would ride into the city in his chariot, pulled by a white horse. Singers danced, banners waved, trumpets blew. The booty was carted behind. The crowds shouted and jeered the prisoners of war chained to the chariot along with the conquered king. Paul uses that picture to demonstrate Jesus' triumph over Satan at the cross. When Jesus bore our sins, guilt and shame in His body on the cross, He left Satan, the accuser, with nothing to accuse! Satan can't accuse us as law-breakers because Jesus was accused for us. God shamed Satan as the supposed destroyer of the Son of Man by raising Christ from the dead. The Apostle John wrote, *"Jesus came to destroy the works of the devil."* (1 John 3:8) Here is the other side of the Christian message. Yes, we bring only our sin and guilt to Jesus at the cross, and see our whole lives in that light. But, we also are fully advantaged by the empty tomb to live in the victory of the resurrection moment by moment.

[10]And in Him you have been made complete, and He is the head of all rule and authority; [11]and in Him you were also circumcised with a circumcision made without hands, in the removal of the body of the flesh by the circumcision of Christ; [12]having been buried with Him in baptism, in which you were also raised up with Him through faith in the working of God, who raised Him from the dead. [13]And when you were dead in your transgressions and the uncircumcision of your flesh, He made you alive together with Him, having forgiven us all our transgressions, [14]having cancelled out the certificate of debt consisting of decrees against us and which was hostile to us; and He has taken it out of the way, having nailed it to the cross. [15]When He had disarmed the rulers and authorities, He made a public display of them, having triumphed over them through Him.

Colossians 2:10-15

A Heart Free from Sin

"We're not struggling to be free, but we are free to struggle."

The game of golf mirrors life: everyone playing golf, universally, sooner than later, much more frequently than not, does something they wish they hadn't or does not do something they wish they had. That's like life: we all do things we don't want to do; we don't do things we want to do. We battle the impulses of our sinful desires. We struggle to master self-control: to do repeatedly what we know is the right thing to do. The answer in golf, of course, is to buy new clubs, better golf balls or take lessons! Perhaps that will shave strokes off your game.

What is the answer in life? Now that's an important question. Battling indwelling sin may be a matter of despair—or true salvation joy. The false teachers in Colossae—winsomely and persuasively—said, "We have the secret to mastering the flesh. Pass through our special rites of initiation, follow special regulations, and then you will control your desires." Paul's response to that in Colossians 2:11-15 is simply: *that is not Christianity*!

Christianity is not moral self-improvement, living by the right rules. Christianity is not a morally retrained heart, but rather a supernaturally changed heart. You only get the right behavior for the right reasons out of a heart Jesus Christ fills with His Spirit.

So notice Paul's argument: the false teachers proscribe, according to Col. 2:23, a *"self-imposed religion that has no value against the indulgence of the flesh."* Rules may for a time restrain the heart, but ultimately don't change it. The good news is, because of your faith in Christ, you are united to Christ (*"in Him"*) and thus all of the benefits of Jesus' perfect obedience, death and resurrection are freely yours. Do you hear Paul saying, "Don't let the false teachers take you captive to their warped philosophy and techniques for a morally restrained heart?" You're filled (v. 10) completely for the meeting of every spiritual need.

You're also free—from the *penalty of sin* by the death of Jesus, from the *power of the law* (God wiped the legal debt clean), from the *power of Satan* (whom God disarmed at the cross), and from the *power of sin* by the indwelling Spirit.

Our focus is verses 11 and 12. This is the Magna Carta of Christian freedom, what Paul calls the *circumcision done without hands* that spiritually transforms the heart indwelt by God's power. Let's answer two questions. What is the circumcision made without hands? What difference does it make for you?

What is the circumcision made without hands?

In order to understand the *"circumcision made without hands,"* an obviously spiritual operation, we need to first explore its predecessor in the history of redemption, the circumcision done with hands. God initiated in the old covenant an outward sign of belonging among His people: the circumcision of the male foreskin. The following biblical references help us understand the meaning and dimensions of it for believers.

It was *instituted* by God in Genesis 17 as a sign of the covenant of grace. *"This is my covenant, which you shall keep, between me and you and your offspring after you: Every male among you shall be circumcised. You shall be circumcised in the flesh of your foreskins, and it shall be a sign of the covenant between me and you..."* (Gen. 17:10)

It is *essential* to membership in the community of God's people. *"Any uncircumcised male who is not circumcised in the flesh of his foreskin shall be cut off from his people; he has broken covenant."* (Gen. 17:14) *"Thus says the Lord God: O house of Israel, enough of your abominations, in admitting foreigners, uncircumcised in heart and flesh to be in my sanctuary, profaning my temple..."* (Ezek. 44:6-7)

It *signifies* the new heart God alone gives by grace. *"...If then their uncircumcised heart is humbled and they make amends for their iniquity, then I will remember my covenant..."* (Lev. 26:41) *"Circumcise therefore the foreskin of your heart, and be no longer stubborn..."* (Deut. 10:16) *"And the Lord your God will circumcise your heart and the heart of your offspring, so that you will love the Lord your God with all your heart and with all your soul, that you may live."* (Deut. 30:6) *"Circumcise yourselves to the Lord; remove the foreskin of your hearts..."* (Jer. 4:4) *"... The Lord has not given you a heart to understand or eyes to see or ears to hear."* (Deut. 29:4)

It is *useless* without the inner reality to which it pointed. *"Behold, days are coming, declares the Lord, when I will punish all those who are circumcised merely in the flesh—Egypt, Judah, Edom, Ammon, Moab...for all these nations are uncircumcised, and all the house of Israel is uncircumcised in heart."* (Jer. 9:25-26) *"To whom shall I speak and give warning, that they may hear? Behold, their ears are uncircumcised, they cannot listen; behold, the word of the Lord is to them an object of scorn; they take no pleasure in it."* (Jer. 6:10) *"For no one is a Jew who is merely one outwardly, nor is circumcision outward and physical. But a Jew is one inwardly, and circumcision is a matter of the heart, by the Spirit, not by the letter. His praise is not from man but from God."* (Romans 2:28-29)

It *symbolizes* the promises of the gospel:

> *cleansing:* Jesus is cut off for us (Is. 53:8) *"By oppression and judgment he was taken away; and as for his generation, who considered that he was cut off from the*

land of the living, stricken for the transgression of my people."

consecration: the Father receives us as His People

renewal: the Spirit gives a new heart

It is *replaced* by water baptism. Paul seems to be saying, "If you want a rite of initiation, you've already had it! You were baptized." Circumcision, the rite of initiation into the community of faith, is now, in the new covenant, replaced by a bloodless, gender-neutral sign: water baptism.

It is *revealed* as the *circumcision of the heart* by Christ. *"In Him also you were circumcised with a circumcision made without hands, by putting off the body of the flesh, by the circumcision of Christ..."* (Col. 2:11) *"We know that our old self was crucified with him in order that the body of sin might be brought to nothing, so that we would no longer be enslaved to sin."* (Rom. 6:6) *"Wretched man that I am! Who will deliver me from this body of death? Thanks be to God through Jesus Christ our Lord!"* (Rom. 7:24) *"For we are the real circumcision, who worship by the Spirit of God and glory in Christ Jesus and put no confidence in the flesh..."* (Phil. 3:3)

The circumcision of Christ is His gracious work in us, by His Spirit, coming to dwell in us, cutting away indwelling sin and bringing us life and newness of heart.

What difference does this make for you?

This is your truest identity. Faith sees oneself as new in Christ. You should never think of yourself as a religious person, but as a renewed person. We live with a supernaturally changed heart. Never think of yourself as a slave to sin, but a person with free, full access to Christ's resurrection power. It isn't even proper to call a person in union with Christ a sinner. From the Bible's perspective, we are now saints who sin. This is how we ought to view any other believer, as well.

What about those who are outside of Christ? Should we look at others as unclean, as if we have reason to boast in ourselves? We need to see others as slaves to sin, and therefore desperate for our compassion and in need of the gospel. The only reason we're not in their shoes is the grace of Christ. Don't expect much from a slave to sin. Pray for God to set him free. Because of a believer's union with Christ, there is hope for change. God has given you an unceasing fountain of grace for power to change. Slow progress, even regress, should not be grounds for condemnation, but rather humbling ourselves before the Lord. Such power is accessed primarily in prayer by appropriating God's word in our hearts.

It follows, finally, that you must scrutinize your desires. One of the ways we change is to examine our desires, for all behavior springs from desire. Why do I want what I want? How is my behavior fulfilling my desires? We often find our desires competing fiercely with our priorities. The key is to line those up together. God has given us a new heart so that we will desire Christ above all other things.

[1]Whoever believes that Jesus is the Christ is born of God; and whoever loves the Father loves the child born of Him. [2]By this we know that we love the children of God, when we love God and observe His commandments. [3]For this is the love of God, that we keep His commandments; and His commandments are not burdensome. [4]For whatever is born of God overcomes the world; and this is the victory that has overcome the world—our faith. [5]And who is the one who overcomes the world, but he who believes that Jesus is the Son of God?

1 John 5:1-5

A Heart Free from the Law

"You can only keep the law once you realize you can't keep it."

I'm not sure if this should be considered true confessions, or simply a point of interest, but twelve years ago, I had only a passing interest in golf. I was addicted to basketball, but regarding golf—I could take it or leave it. Then, I came under its power. The golf bug bit. My heart awakened to the absolute magic of golf. And with that awakening came new desires: to play more, to improve aspects of the game, to watch it on TV, to have better golf balls and clubs—you get the idea, new desires abounded that I never even envisioned before golf was awakened in me.

So it is with faith. When faith awakens in us, new desires necessarily follow. John is showing that in this text. Why is that necessary? Lot's of people in the churches John addressed claimed to have faith, but they didn't all live it out with the same faithfulness. Apparently, their faith was not accompanied by new desires. So how do you tell true possession of faith from mere profession of faith in Jesus Christ?

John reveals that faith changes you; it creates new desires. You recognize true belief in Jesus by its power to create new loves. John has already demonstrated the power of perfect love—it casts out fear and hatred. (1 John 4:18) This text shows the power of faith to create new loves in us, which we otherwise wouldn't naturally have.

What is faith?

According to 1 John 5:1, faith is *believing that Jesus is the Christ*. Notice how verse 5 repeats that idea: faith is *believing that Jesus is the Son of God*. Faith is fixated on a person—Jesus of Nazareth—like radar in a fighter jet locks on a target. Faith acknowledges the facts about Him—He is the Son of God, the Messiah—and trusts personally in what He came to do: save sinners from the penalty and power of sin.

Faith lays hold of Jesus, trusting that He alone is sufficient to make us perfect for God's holy presence. Think of yourself drowning in a torrential river. You're about to go under. Someone throws you a life preserver from the shoreline. What do you do? You lay hold of it with all your might; you grab it. You place the weight of your life upon it. That's believing, or faith. We abandon our own efforts at deliverance from death, and rely exclusively on (rest upon) Jesus, the lifesaver.

Faith contributes nothing. Suppose I spent five thousand dollars at an exquisite furniture maker and bought you a cherry corner cupboard. I delivered it to your home, and there it stood in your dining room in all its glory. Do you need to add anything to it? Would you start sanding, cutting the wood or adding glue or finish? Of course not! What I delivered was finished, in perfect form; you simply receive it as is! So, too, our salvation in Christ; it matters not what we're like when we accept the gift of salvation. By faith, sinful people freely exchange their guilt for the perfection of God. The soul that has nothing freely draws upon the inexhaustible riches of God. How much faith do I need? Whether it is a frail, weak hand that slowly moves the meat to the mouth, or a swift muscular arm, it's not the strength of the hand but the goodness of the meat that saves.

Where does faith come from? God. Faith comes from *being born of God*. God quickens the heart by His Spirit; He *persuades* the heart of the danger of sin, *convincing* us of the righteous judgment of God, and *enables* us to believe that Jesus lovingly accepts us. We willingly come to Christ because He makes us willing! Faith is the gift of God. If you have it, thank Him; if you don't, ask Him for it. He always gives it to those who ask, having never turned away one person in the history of man.

So how do you know you have faith? At one level, it's very subjective: the Spirit witnesses to your heart that you believe. At another level, faith objectively produces new loves.

What new loves does faith produce?

1. *Love for God as Father, "whoever loves the Father…"* (1 John 5:1) Loving the Father is the result of believing that Jesus is the Son of God, the Messiah. Jesus is God's Son by the Father's designation. The gospel reveals the Father's giving heart: He gave His only son. Thus, no longer is God some impersonal force, or an old man who can stay preoccupied way out in the universe, or simply your Creator, or worse, a Judge to fear. Faith sees the goodness of God in sending His son to die for you, that you could be His child. The *only* worship, honor and devotion God wants is as a giving Father. In the gospel He says, "Love me as a Father who begets. My Son Jesus is my only begotten, the first born of all creation, the first born among many brothers, my beloved, in whom I am well pleased. My Son was begotten in time so you too could become my begotten ones, born of my will by my Spirit for my glory and pleasure."

2. *Love for those born of God, "whoever loves the Father loves the one born of Him"* (1 John 5:1b) God says to you, "Son, you love me, right?" Yes, Father. "Well, you see your fellow believer?" Yes. "He's my son too, love him, love him like you want Me to love you." That's the right reason to love a fellow believer. Love him *not* for what he might do for you, or because you happen to find him agreeable, or because he is so gifted, but because God holds him in His hand and cherishes him.

How, then, do you know you're loving people the way God wants you to? John answers that in verse 2, *"by this we know that we love the children of God, when we love God and keep His commandments."* In other words, the best thing I can do for you is first, love God. Parents, do you want to love your children? Fall deeply in love with Jesus. Wives, do you want to shower your husband with affection? First, fall deeply in love with Jesus. Get His love fully in your heart. The result? He'll control you. He'll fill you with wisdom, affection, patience, kindness—all of which make your love for others exactly what they need.

With whom would you rather live: a person in love with himself or a person in love with God? A person driven by grace and gratitude, or one driven by ambition and lust? A person you notice is *so* thankful for what he has, who thinks like a debtor—that he owes others service—or a person who is a vacuum of self-concern?

Verse 2 is teaching that we love others best when we keep God's commandments. That means we should always set up a five-sided frame when we look at another person. The five sides define how we will treat them. Side 1: don't murder (sixth commandment). Side 2: don't sexually abuse (seventh commandment). Side 3: don't steal (eighth commandment). Side 4: don't lie (ninth commandment). Side 5: don't covet anything they have, but give a blessing (tenth commandment).

See the point? You can *never* hurt another or yourself by obeying God's law. You can *only* promote their welfare and your own by obeying God's law. You will *always* glorify God by keeping His commands. That brings us to the third new love faith creates.

3. *Love for God's values.* That's at the heart of the tension between the values of the world and our faith, those things that we deem important. The world has a way of thinking, originating in the liar, the devil, which excludes God's revelation. The world is a value system that marginalizes God—it doesn't need His help. You find it often in a culture's catch phrases. Be true to yourself. If it

feels good do it. Look out for #1. The one who dies with the most toys, wins. You deserve a break today. As long as you're sincere, it doesn't matter what you believe. I'm the captain of my own ship, the master of my own fate.

The world's values are an attempt to make sense out of life apart from God. The soul is grabbing pride, possessions, appearances, pleasures or power to make life bearable. These things are not the problem per se, but rather, it is our attitude and motives concerning them. Do they rule us? When we're denied them, are we like a caged lion? They are all very appealing. What power can resist them? Verse 5 asks, *"Who is the one who overcomes the world but he who believes that Jesus is the Son of God?"* Faith, as a weapon of warfare with the allure of the world, is only as effective as its firm hold on Jesus.

Faith will move you to serve Jesus in ways you never expected. I've experienced this. I mentioned that twelve years ago I had only a passing interest in golf; well I had no interest whatsoever in leaving family and friends in my home state of Virginia. I had to ask God to give me the faith to venture out. He did, and He brought about an opportunity. Four families were praying for a church planter to go to Ft. Worth TX, to help start a PCA church. By the grace of God, and the faith He gave, I ventured out and God planted a church.

The last new love to examine which faith creates is one that often surprises us.

4. *New love for God's law.* Christianity is not merely a pronouncement: you're forgiven! It isn't simply receiving a new nametag; "Mike Sharrett, he once was lost but now is found." That's all true, of course, but there's more. Christianity is a personal transformation. 2 Cor. 5:14 says, *"If anyone is in Christ he is a new creation."* Ezekiel 11:19 tells us, *"God will take out the old heart and put in a new one."* Romans 6:6 confirms, the *old man died, the body of sin has been rendered powerless.*

One of the most dramatic changes is our relationship to the law of God. The Spirit gives you power to obey God and a new attitude toward His commandments. Look again at what John says in 1 John 5:3, *"For this is the love of God"* (our love for God, because He first loved us) *"that we keep His commandments,"* echoing his writings in John 14:15.

But John doesn't stop there. He editorializes, as it were, regarding faith's new attitude toward God's commandments. *"And His commandments are not burdensome"* (irksome, oppressive). Really? Can you honestly say that? You can by the faith that embraces all that Jesus is for you! This isn't so much a statement about us (an indicative) as it is about the glory of God revealed in Christ. Only in Christ, through faith, by Christ's Spirit, can anyone say, and *mean, "His commandments are not burdensome."* That statement reveals the power of grace.

Those of you who own a business have power to command your employees to do tasks. The order itself, however, doesn't guarantee they will *want* to perform a certain task. And you probably don't care. You just want the job done well. But God commands His will and has the power to insure obedience in people who *want* to please Him, who find the work delightful—hard, maybe, but not irksome. God, who does all things well, not only wants the job done well, but He wants those doing it to savor the reason. Only God can get you to do the right thing for the right reason.

Isn't that where you want to live? Not only possessing the power to do what you know is right and good, but also possessing the desire to please the Father. How do you get there? The key is seeing the glory of Christ. How do we get to the place where we see the glory of Christ in such a way that the quality of our obedience is radically new?

We begin with a foggy view of the law.

The place we all naturally begin is with a flawed or foggy understanding of the law. Depending on your upbringing and life circumstances, some of you avoid it. You don't care to be confronted with its standards; you'd prefer to live autonomously, to "be true to yourself." Perhaps that's because you burned out trying to be a good person and gave up. What's the use? It's too hard. Sin is pleasurable, not to mention addictive. When the day is over you have to admit you have no power to obey. Do you see that under this scenario you are a slave to your passions? They can't be constrained by the law.

Others of us use the law to justify ourselves. Typically, this person looks superficially at the law, compares himself to really bad people and concludes, "I'm a good person." You invariably build a record, a legal reputation and probably feel good about yourself. Do you see the danger? You obey God to feel good about yourself—for self-gratification, to appear competent, to make yourself look good. You ultimately just want to be known as a good person. To live here you have to live in the fog, both not clearly seeing how far you miss God's standard nor clearly seeing what the standard is. You inflate your ability to be righteous, and deflate the "heart demand" of the law. Such folks tend to chafe under the law. You do only what's required, like the athlete in practice who runs and sprints hard only when the coach is looking. You grind out your duty, only to perform grudgingly. God's demands infringe on your agenda and desires. Obedience is a burden. You keep trying and won't give up because that's wrong; you're the energizer bunny, still going, but no joy! You usually fear that God will judge you; your guilt is tremendous and the law is a terror.

Faith sees the glory of Jesus.

Wherever you are, your view of God's law is flawed and foggy, because you lack faith. The place you need to be is where faith sees the glory of Jesus. The glory of Jesus burns away our foggy views of God's law. What is that glory? First, the beauty of the law was lived out perfectly in Jesus; He fulfilled it's every demand, to the letter and by the right Spirit. Jesus did not do anything grudgingly. It was His delight to obey His Father, though no doubt it was extremely difficult and painful. Since the law reveals the character of God, we know the incarnation of that character in Jesus. He is conviction without intimidation, gentleness without weakness, compassion without sentimentalism, truth without harshness, peace without passivity, joy without triviality, anger without capriciousness.

Second, Jesus bore the curse of law breaking in our place. Our sense of dread under God's law comes from our guilt of unfulfilled obligation. Stop trying to anesthetize your guilt with pleasures or substances. See in Jesus the only one who can lift that burden from you; He extracts from the law the sting of death (1 Cor. 15:55-56). His blood turns the bitter waters of our guilt into the sweet cup of salvation. Maybe your whole life you have sensed the law screaming at you—haunting, harassing, exposing, condemning— and it should, it was designed to do so! But under the cross, you can hear, with the ears of faith, Jesus shout, *"Silence!"* He hushed the law's loud thunder.

Third, Jesus pours His heart-transforming power into us. Jesus, having bought you for Himself, smiles upon His beloved, jealous to pour into your heart all the grace and mercy necessary to enable you to obey Him. Do you see the multi-faceted dimensions of God's grace to you in Christ? By Jesus' perfect obedience, you receive *justifying* grace. By Jesus' death, you receive *saving* grace. By Jesus' Spirit, you receive *renewing* grace.

The final place faith brings us is to the point of embracing the law for the right reason. The law is not burdensome or irksome, though obedience may prove exceedingly challenging due to the presence of indwelling sin. Again, as we see the glory of Christ, the most beautiful person in all the world, and He loves us—imagine that!—we begin to desire all that He has promised. We want to be home with Him in glory. And we want to get there safely, not recklessly in self-indulgence, but judiciously, as only Jesus can wisely proscribe. Doesn't He humble us to admit we don't know the way unless He shows us? Then the law will be a *"lamp unto my feet and a light unto my path."* (Ps. 119:105) If you've ever needed to walk out of an extremely dangerous place in the darkness of night, you'd be eternally thankful for a lantern—even if it were heavy, or smelled of kerosene, or gave your hand a blister, or it was a challenge to carry. But not for an instant is it irksome or irritating—it shows the way to safety—a small price to pay! So too, the law of God.

Jesus said in Matt. 11:28-30, *"Come unto Me, all who are weary and heavy-laden, and I will give you rest. Take My yoke upon you, and learn from Me, for I am gentle and humble in heart: and you shall find rest for your souls. For My yoke is easy and My burden is light."* So with the eyes of faith we see that God's law isn't arbitrary, but intended for our good. It reveals Him to us; it makes us more like Him. And it explains how to bless others, and not stand in their way of seeing God's glory in Christ. Thus, when we know His love, we don't feel coerced to obey, as if under undue pressure, but we feel free to love Him, even despite our constant failures and innate frailty. The law will provoke you to sin, actually, but not because it is bad, but rather because sin is incited by it.

Paul's experience with the law.

Paul's testimony in Romans 7:7-12 provides a rich examination of how our relationship to God's law changes. *"[7]What shall we say then? Is the law sin? May it never be! On the contrary, I would not have come to know sin except through the law; for I would not have known about coveting if the law had not said, 'You shall not covet'. [8]But sin, taking opportunity through the commandment, produced in me coveting of every kind; for apart from the law sin is dead. [9]And I was once alive apart from the law; but when the commandment came, sin became alive, and I died; [10]and this commandment, which was to result in life, proved to result in death for me; [11]for sin, taking opportunity through the commandment, deceived me, and through it killed me. [12]So then, the Law is holy, and the commandment is holy and righteous and good..."*

In its context, Paul is answering an objection from his detractors that he doesn't value the law. Why their concern? Because he has just stated in the preceding verses that we have *died to the law* and therefore we *are released from the law.* (Rom. 7:6) That kind of language really concerns folks who have a high regard for the law of God. It sounds like the heresy called Antinomianism, a teaching that holds that since we are saved by grace it doesn't matter what we do, because grace is always greater than our sin. And that's true, at a certain level. In Christ, His grace always outruns our sin! But Paul has addressed this in Romans 6, arguing that the person who wants to go on sinning really isn't united to Christ by faith. When we believe the gospel, our relationship to sin changes. In Romans 7, Paul wants to show that our relationship to the law changes, as well. He is showing that because of the believer's union with Christ, the demands of the law of God were fully, completely and finally met by Jesus upon His death. We are released from the law as the legal stipulation that God requires for everyone to come into His presence. We are released because Jesus has met every single demand of the law; He gave to God perfectly every ounce of righteousness required for His holy presence.

So, in verse 7, Paul wonders aloud if that means the law is somehow bad or sinful. His answer is a resounding *no! "I would not have come to know sin except through the law."* Paul says the law's function in our salvation is to show us our sin. He chronicles here his own experience of discovering the gravity of the law and its condemning power, moving from levity near the law to gravity under its condemning power. Do you see yourself in any of these stages of progression?[*]

Stage 1: "I was once alive apart from the law." (v. 9) The law is inconsequential. Paul means that he felt good about himself, was

---

[*] I am indebted to Tim Keller's study guide on Romans for the following material.

untroubled by the demands of the law, thus fashioning himself a very good person. In this condition, *"sin is dead."* (v. 8) He may have possessed a general sense of right and wrong, had superficial obedience to God, but had no real internal battles with sin because he was at peace with sin.

Stage 2: "But when the commandment came, sin became alive and I died." (v. 9) Paul records a time in his life when he begins to feel the gravity of the law. The deeper intent of the law, going to the heart and to our motives, exposing us as idolaters, hit home with him in the tenth commandment *"I would not have known about coveting if the law had not said, 'You shall not covet'."* (v. 7) Coveting can't be externalized. It exposes our desires as being driven for ourselves and against God. Paul came to see *he* was the problem! He says, *"I died and sin sprang to life."* The cheerful, "I'm OK, you're OK" Pharisee died and sin within him sprang into action.

Stage 3: "This commandment, which was to result in life, proved to result in death for me." (v. 10) Paul now realizes he can't use the law to justify himself. Yes, it was originally given for Adam and Eve to obtain life before God. But since sin entered the world, we are all unable to keep the law unto life—everyone except Jesus! Now Paul feels the condemnation of the law—he's guilty and helpless! Now when sin and the law meet, they conspire within him to disobedience. *"For sin, taking opportunity through the commandment, deceived me, and through it killed me…"* (v. 11)

Stage 4: "So then, the Law is holy, and the commandment is holy and righteous and good." (v. 12) Once converted, Paul sees the value of the law. It not only convicts him of sin, but it also shows him how to love the Jesus who saved him. Now he can use the law for the right reason.

Short of a grace-driven obedience to the law, we will never give to God the obedience He desires. Until the gospel fuels our sense of pleasing God, out of gratitude and for His glory, our attempts at conformity to God's high and holy standards will consistently miss the mark. Have you experienced the joy of obedience, simply for Christ's sake? When you do, your instinct is to thank Him for it, not taking credit yourself, but finding delight in His power, transforming you from weakness to strength.

Your understanding of the law of God is critical to gaining eternal life. If we may make a sweeping generalization, there are ultimately only two kinds of people in the world: those trying to establish their *own* righteousness before God and those trusting in the righteousness of *another*. Those who are trying to establish their *own* righteousness usually fit one of four types.

Those who think they are succeeding. These are people who view themselves as really good people. They have great disdain for bad people. They don't necessarily have to be religious. They invariably are proud, judgmental and unsympathetic to "losers."

Those who aren't so sure they're as righteous as they should be. These folks have a more tender conscience, admit to the high standard God requires and try hard to do the right thing. But because they know they fail sometimes, they wonder if they've done enough. These folks, consequently, live with varying levels of anxiety and uncertainty. Their sense of failing themselves may express itself in anger toward others or shyness.

Those who know they'll never *be righteous enough.* Here are people with a pretty good sense of *what's right and I'm wrong.* Perhaps they have failed enough in life (or have been told repeatedly they are worthless) that they know they will never be what God requires. These are the kind of people Jesus said were actually quite close to the kingdom of God. This is close to being *"poor in spirit."* (Matt. 5:3) People who have no sense of ever really measuring up will, eventually, become hopeless. They will do something to numb their existential pain.

Those who seek to compensate for their lack of moral perfection with a religious supplement. I talk to many, many people who say they believe in Jesus, but their Jesus is like a ladder.

Because they just aren't tall enough morally, they step on the "Jesus ladder" which makes heaven within reach. Their salvation is a combination of their own righteousness, plus Jesus. Are you in this group? Is your Jesus someone who helps those who help themselves? The Bible says all you contribute to salvation is sin. Jesus does it all; He doesn't need anything from you. He is the whole show. His perfect life and His sacrificial death, received by faith, are sufficient to fit you for heaven. The book of Galatians was written explicitly to counter this kind of thinking.

To those who are trusting in the righteousness of *another*, the gospel of Jesus Christ is good news. Jesus does for us what we are unable to do for ourselves. He is called the blessed hope, for good reason. Those hopeless of ever being good enough receive perfect righteousness as a gift of grace. *"God made Him who knew no sin to become sin on our behalf, that we might become the righteousness of God in Him."* (2 Cor. 5:21) *The* question of religion is, "Who can make people righteous?" Jesus is the only one. Our confidence is in Him. *"But by His doing you are in Christ Jesus, who became to us wisdom from God, and righteousness and sanctification, and redemption, that, just as it is written, 'Let him who boasts, boast in the Lord.'"* (1 Cor. 1:30-31) You know these kinds of people by their hope, peace, confidence, humility, gratitude, compassion and sense of purpose.

PART III

THE HEART AT WAR

[1]If then you have been raised up with Christ, keep seeking the things above, where Christ is, seated at the right hand of God. [2]Set your mind on the things above, not on the things that are on earth. [3]For you have died and your life is hidden with Christ in God. [4]When Christ, who is our life, is revealed, then you also will be revealed with Him in glory.

Colossians 3:1-4

The Heart Set Above

"The heart always follows the mind."

When my daughter played softball, I usually sat behind the backstop to keep score for the coaches. I liked that vantage point because it gave me a perfect view of the pitches coming across home plate. I can't tell you how many times I've watched perfect pitches sail right down the middle and the batter doesn't flinch an inch; she stands there like a statue, apparently not even noticing the ball! As you might imagine, I'm silently screaming inside, "What are you thinking?" I mean that literally. A huge part of batting is thinking: attitude, expectation and assumptions. I tried to teach my daughter, when you step into the batter's box, look at the pitcher and think, "Give me a pitch I can hit!" In other words, expect to hit the ball, assume you're going to swing, adopt a *hitter's attitude.* Some batters think, "I hope the ball doesn't hit me; I'll probably strike out; I'll just wait for four balls and try to get a walk." They should think, give me a pitch I can hit. Why? The body follows the mind.

Now I'm not writing to give you batting lessons. But the same principle applies to life: attitude and thinking is critical. Your conduct follows your mind; your thinking determines your emotions. It often feels like our emotions direct our behavior; but the truth is, your belief system and your thoughts determine what you do. This is incredibly vital because we all battle the impulses of indwelling sin, and we need to employ the right strategy to have victory. The broader context, going back into Colossians 2, assumes we will all be assaulted by sinful desires. It is inevitable. The Christian is a person who has a new relationship to God *and* a new relationship to sin. Yes, the penalty of sin is paid and the power of sin is broken; but the presence of sin is still very much alive. Peter says in his first epistle, *"Abstain from fleshly lusts which wage war against the soul."* (1 Peter 2:11) Paul warns in Galatians 5:17 that the *flesh wars against the spirit*. How, then, can sinful desires be subdued? This is one of the most pressing issues for a person seeking to honor Jesus Christ. If you are serious in your pursuit of Christ, you will inevitably find yourself crying out in humble frustration with Paul, *"I am not practicing what I would like to do, but I am doing the very thing I hate..."* (Rom. 7:15)

In Colossae, the false teachers promoted rules, secret visions, ascetic practices and various religious rites for the perfecting of the spirit. But Paul, in Col. 2:23, flat out denies that rules have any value for restraining the impulses of the flesh. The heart is what counts. Bad rules should be ignored; good rules can't, in themselves, control the flesh. What, then, can restrain the powerful, unceasing impulses of the flesh? Paul says to subdue sin you need to *think*. It's not about feelings or sheer will power or techniques. Thinking is the key to behavior; therefore, thinking is the key to holiness. In these four verses Paul outlines three directions to think: think *up* (Col. 3:1-2), think *back* (3:3), think *forward* (3:4). We discover, not surprisingly, that each direction God calls us to think, we find Jesus.

Think up

Verses 1 and 2 contain two imperatives. Verse 1 counsels to *keep seeking* (the things above). To seek means to aspire to or aim at. Verse 2 advises *set your mind* (on the things above). The idea is "to be intent upon" or "give mind to." There are at least three principles inherent in these two imperatives.

1. Thinking up must be an on-going activity, a way of living.

Both verbs are in the present tense, calling for continuous activity. If you don't consciously and deliberately think up, you will invariably think down. Sin never takes a vacation from tempting you to think ungodly thoughts. You have to pack truth into your mind and *keep* packing it in. Thinking up is like raising your hand to block the glaring sun behind a person with whom you're speaking. You have to decide to raise your hand, and make an effort to keep it there, otherwise your hand naturally rests limp at your side. The only way to see the person is to use your hand as an instrument to keep the glare from blinding you. Likewise with thinking up. Our minds do not naturally stay fixed on the right stuff; they tend to drift, according to verse 2, to the *"things of the earth."* Paul is not giving in to a Platonic dualism—matter is bad and spirit is good. He is indicating that an earthbound mindset is one that sees reality without God in the picture. The things of this world are catalogued in verses 5 and 8.

Is this hard to do? Yes! But look at the reward. *"To set the mind on the flesh is death, but to set the mind on the Spirit is life and peace. For the mind set on the flesh is hostile to God, for it does not submit to God's law; indeed, it cannot."* (Rom. 8:6-7) God's word shows us that, when you break it down, most of your anxiety is faulty thinking; most of your anger is faulty thinking. Most of your impatience is faulty thinking; most of your bitterness is faulty thinking.

2. Thinking up embraces our identity in Christ.

The most peaceful, joyful, selfless believers are those who think long and hard about truth, doctrine, and specifically, who they are in Christ. That's why Paul begins the section, *"If then you have been raised up with Christ..."* (Col. 3:1) What's that? *"Raised up with Christ"* is the status of every believer; it is union with Christ. Your faith unites you to Christ, so that what is true of Him is true of you. When God raised His Son from the dead, Jesus rose to a realm where sin has no dominion. The same is true of you. Paul unpacks this in Rom. 6:1-6.

The point here is, before Paul gives the imperatives of the Christian life (what you should *do*), he first sets forth the indicative, the "what is," the fact of who you *are* as a person in Christ. In other words, never think of yourself as a slave to sin. Never think of yourself as needing to prove anything to God. Never think of yourself as struggling to be free, but as free to struggle. Never think of yourself as an orphan in this world.

I remember when I tried out for the varsity football team in high school. I wasn't sure if I'd be on the JV or varsity, but once I was declared quarterback on varsity, and received the varsity jersey, I never doubted my status. In Christ, God declares us His precious, forgiven sons and daughters, and clothes us with the righteous jersey of Jesus' moral perfection. But, you protest, that sounds so detached from my experience. What seem all too real are my sinful urges. Plus, what are *the things above*? (v. 2) That sounds vague. Will I be so heavenly minded that I'm no earthly good? Paul defines *"the things above"* as *"where Christ is, seated at the right hand of the Father."* (v. 1) *Keep seeking* that place as your ambition. *Set your mind* on that place, exclusively, and constantly.

3.   Thinking up looks to the things above.

What is so special about that place? What about it truly helps in temptation? *Jesus is there. He* is the most glorious person in the universe—the radiance and splendor of God. To look upon Him is to behold pure moral excellence, unconditional love, awe-striking kindness, undefiled holiness.

Jesus is seated. That means He finished His work. The Father sent Him to earth on a business trip. For 33 years, He earned, for His people, a salvation that can't be taken away; He decisively, once for all, put away the sins of all who believe in Him. He *"made purification for sins"* (Heb. 1:3). If you were dying of thirst and found a case of Ozarka bottled water, you wouldn't put yourself at serious risk of dehydration and first boil it! It's already purified. Jesus sat down at the Father's right hand, having made purification for your sins. If you trust Jesus, you can't get any more purification than you already have! He rose victorious, ascended to His Father, and the Father said, "Sit down, job well done. Now we'll pour out the Spirit upon all the people I'm giving you as your family. All that's left to do is for them to receive the gift."

Jesus is reigning. Paul's allusion to *the right hand of the Father* picks up the imagery of Psalm 110. We are to picture a throne, a bench on which two are seated, as it were, in honor and glory. Jesus has triumphed as Divine Warrior, and God has given to Him power and authority to rule the universe. In that rule, Jesus blesses and helps His own. So when Paul says look up, he means, when you view your trials, struggles or losses, never do so but through the lens or perspective of Jesus' rule over all things. He will provide for you, why fear man? Why not love your enemy; God is on your side?

Jesus is praying. The right hand of the Father is the place of intercession. *"Jesus Christ is at the right hand of the Father, who indeed is interceding for us."* (Rom. 8:34) *"He is able to save to the uttermost those who draw near to God through him, since he always lives to make intercession for them."* (Heb. 7:25) Paul says, to think *up* is to tell yourself, no matter how you feel or what you've done, Jesus is praying for you. "Oh, but surely not when I fail! Doesn't He turn His face away?" On the contrary. Remember Jesus' word to Peter. *"Satan has requested to sift you like wheat, but I will pray for you."* (Luke 22:31) Wasn't Peter's denial of Jesus the occasion for Jesus to pray for Peter?

Think back

"You have died and your life is hidden with Christ in God." (Col. 3:3) The two verbs here draw a profound contrast. *You have died* is past tense, an aorist (Greek verb form), an action happening one time in the past. *You are hidden* is present tense, an indicative, simply telling it like it is. God keeps you continuously hidden in His Son. This is Paul's logic for moral change: be who you are. God has made you something, so act consistent with that! Act in accordance with two unchangeable truths about yourself: *you died; your life is hidden.* When sin tempts you astray, it always hides those glorious facts.

You died. Really? When? When you were united to Christ by faith. The old you, the person born in Adam, a slave to sin, a pawn of Satan, unbelieving and ignorant, that person is dead. That person, who lived under condemnation and the power of sin, who lived with *self* as king, was nailed to the cross, crucified with

121

Christ. *"I have been crucified with Christ, and it is no longer I who live, but Christ lives in me..."* (Gal. 2:20) When that person died, the Holy Spirit brought a new man to life in you. If Jesus was not raised from the dead, no one could ever change morally. Col. 3:3 says now you have life. (In Greek, the word is *zoe*, spiritual life, the indestructible life of God Himself. For *"we have become partakers of the divine nature"*—2 Peter 1:4). Import that truth into the way you think. Think about the way you think. One of the most helpful things you can do is to stop and think. Think through the consequences of your sins. A professional counselor explained to me how he did this with a man considering suicide. He helped the man run the camera forward to the full, wide-reaching impact of this act so he could see how many others it would profoundly affect.

So train yourself to ask, "What am I telling myself? What am I believing that is making me act this way? Is what I am thinking descriptive of the old man (OM) or the new man (NM)?" For example:

OM (old man): That guy's a jerk and I don't owe him anything.
NM (new man): Jesus, I was your enemy, but now that you've loved me I can show anyone kindness.

OM: If only I had a little bit more money, or a better job, car, house, spouse...then I'd be happy.
NM: Jesus, (always start with Jesus in your thinking!) I'll never be content until I'm deeply satisfied with you.

OM: I must be liked, appreciated, approved by others!
NM: Jesus, it doesn't matter what anyone thinks of me—you the King of the universe call me friend. I am going to spend a lot more time with you than with anyone else.

OM: I need to earn God's favor; I need to do more.
NM: Jesus, because I am hidden in you, God sees me as if I died on the cross, as if I lived your perfect life, as if I did everything you did, as if I am seated with you at His right hand.

OM: Well, just a little bit of sin won't hurt much, after all, I'm forgiven.

NM: Jesus, keep me from every sin, for it is heinous in your sight, and it can only hurt others and me.

OM: I worked hard for what I have and it's mine. I'll do whatever I want with my money.

NM: Jesus, everything I have is because of your grace, so what may I give to you as a thank you?

OM: I'm fearful because I could fail in faith and God might forsake me.

NM: Jesus, I am hidden in you, the place where you long to nourish me intimately, and the place of greatest safety in all the world. If nothing can threaten your status, nothing can threaten mine.

Think forward

What makes investing in the stock market risky? The simple fact is that you don't know the future of any stock. Such crystal ball knowledge of the future would make for incredibly successful choices today. But how totally unrealistic is that? It is, except in the kingdom of Jesus Christ. One of the central principles of Christianity is this: our theology of the future affects our choices for today. Christianity, in other words, boasts of a kind of insider trading. But this trading is all legal, because a good, righteous and all knowing God is at the center of it. Col. 3:4 is insider trading information for the person who belongs to Jesus Christ.

It is a promise about the future meant to determine your choices for today. Everyone's choices today are in some manner determined by their theology of the future. We all have a theology of the future, a belief or assumption about who or what controls the future, and what our final destiny in the future looks like. Some have a baseline joy today because they have great confidence in the future. Some have a baseline anxiety today because the future is very uncertain. Some souls drip with hopelessness because of despair for the future. Some are hedonistic because they believe that when you die you disintegrate.

So why not grab for all the gusto you can get, since you only go around once in life? What does your attitude, countenance, expectation reveal today about your theology of the future?

This is one of the critical questions behind verse 4. Does this seem to be "pie in the sky"? I beg to differ. My parents sacrificed when I was young to pay for my college education years later. Some of you constrain your passions in the now to offer the gift of purity to an unknown spouse in the future. I know a successful businessman who is thinking about seminary courses to take now so he can better serve Christ's kingdom when he retires. Your theology of the future is immensely practical. What does your theology of the future reveal about your attitude today?

Why is Paul raising the question? The context tells us. As we've seen, in verses 1 through 4, Paul explains the objective result of becoming a Christian, the indicative—what you are now in God's eyes because of your faith in Jesus Christ. We see this illustrated in the story of the guy who is stocking grocery shelves when he is called by an NFL team to replace their injured kicker. On Thursday, he is in solidarity with Kroger grocery store making $15,000 a year, but three weeks later, because he is in solidarity with the winner of the Super Bowl, he makes $30,000 for playing in one game! How much *richer* we all are for belonging to Jesus Christ. The Father's reward to the Son of everlasting life is also our reward; the resurrection signifies that God accepts Jesus perfectly forever. The same is true of all who trust in Jesus. They are saved not by their works but by His.

But isn't there a disconnect here in our experience? Yes, Jesus is in the splendor of heaven, but I'm in Virginia! Yes, Jesus is freed from the domain of death, but I'm going to die! Yes, Jesus is immune to all doubt, but not this frail man! There *is* a disconnect in our experience, and verse 4 helps us understand it. What you already are in Christ has not yet been revealed. Look again at verse 4. *"When Christ ... is revealed,* then *you also will be revealed with Him in glory."* The Christian life is a dual trust, a faith about two time periods: the present (believing what God says about my status now), and the future (believing what God says about the eventual

124

disclosing of what I will have)—glory. This is why the text speaks of two revelations: *when* Christ is revealed (a future revelation of Christ) *then* you also will be revealed (a future revelation of you).

What is the future revelation of Jesus Christ? This is commonly called the Second Coming. Jesus promised in many places, *"I will come again."* Why? He came the first time to accomplish the salvation of His people; He will come again to gather them all to Himself. He came the first time offering grace and peace. He will come again in judgment. In John 14:2-3 He promised, *"I go to prepare a place for you, and if I go, I will come again to take you to myself, that where I am, you may be also."*

Some commentators see in this the analogy of a groom coming for his bride. In ancient near eastern culture, a man would betroth himself to his bride, but first go away to prepare a place for them to live. Then he would return for the great wedding feast, and they would go to the prepared place to enjoy each other—'til death do us part. Revelation 19:7f pictures our meeting with the Lord Jesus in heaven as a wedding feast. We anticipate that future event in the Lord's Supper, remembering not only the terms by which we hope to enjoy *His* presence forever—His body and blood offered for us on the cross—but that great joyful feast when Jesus dines with us in glory.

How will this meeting happen? The Bible says every eye will see Him; He will come visibly, bodily, audibly, in like fashion to the way He ascended—on a cloud from heaven. Where? The Bible doesn't say. Apparently, God is capable of revealing the glory of His Son to all the nations at the same time—don't ask me how! When? Jesus said that was a secret, but be prepared. Certain signs may be evident on the earth, but Bible scholars don't agree on all that. Regardless, all believers are agreed that we should be anticipating His return, while doing faithfully everything He wants done. *"Therefore, beloved, since you look for these things, be diligent to be found by Him in peace, spotless and blameless..."* (2 Peter 3:14) The surest way to answer the question of when is, when the harvest is ready. The Second Coming is pictured by Jesus as a final harvest of souls. The church's job between the first and second comings is to proclaim the good news of a Savior for sinners to all the nations. When Jesus has saved all those who from every tribe and tongue will worship Him forever, He will come again to take them to Himself, dealing out retribution and judgment to all who do not believe in Him (2 Thes. 1). He will call forth from the grave all those who have ever lived, pronounce a final judgment on their soul, separate forever those called to eternal life and those who by their sins refused to give God His due. He will destroy this earth and recreate a new heaven and earth, and establish the glory of His everlasting city on the earth, with His presence illuminating it at all times. Satan, death and evil, will be cast into the pit, never to be heard from again. That is a biblical synopsis of the future revelation of Jesus Christ. Do you want in on this? It's all yours for free. Simply ask God to take your sins from you, to give you the gift of eternal life through Christ, to give you a new heart, to give you the grace to repent and embrace Jesus as king of your life.

What does it mean that you will be revealed in glory? *"To be revealed with Him in glory"* (Col. 3:4) means that the indicative will come to full light; what we truly are now, though hidden by sin, will be clearly seen. When the leaves are turning beautiful in the autumn, the true colors, present all the time in the leaf but hidden by the green chlorophyll, are being revealed. Sin, like the chlorophyll, hides the true beauty of who we are now in Christ, until we appear with Him in glory. On that day, we will see the beauty of Jesus Christ perfectly formed in us. *"For I consider that the sufferings of the present time are not worthy to be compared with the glory that is to be revealed to us."* (Rom. 8:18) *"Beloved, now we are children of God, and it had not appeared as yet what we shall be. We know that, when He appears, we shall be like Him, because we shall see Him just as He is."* (1 John 3:2) *"For now we see in a mirror dimly, but then face to face; now I know in part, but then I shall know fully just as I also have been fully known."* (1 Cor. 13:12) In fact, a person united to Jesus Christ is unspeakably glorious. Were we somehow to see each other now as we will be in our glorified state, we would be tempted to fall down and worship each other.

126

What are some implications of this teaching? In the words of Sgt. Joe Friday, "Just the facts, Ma'am!" Stay focused on the facts, not your feelings. We may not often feel justified in God's sight. But the great fact in this verse is *"Christ, who is our* [or your] *life."* (Col. 3:4) That is the indicative. The only reason you would doubt that is if you believed you had to earn it. Another implication: be patient with each other. The world is still under the curse. It doesn't work right yet. We are all a mess. I'm going to let you down, you're going to sin against me, we will misunderstand each other. Nowhere on earth is there perfect communication or perfect life being lived. That is future. But we do have, in the present, resources in the Holy Spirit to give us grace to cope with the ravages of sin. The church is a community where imperfect strugglers are the norm and should be readily accepted. The church should never be a community where differences are left to fester like cancers.

A third implication would be to refrain from spending inordinate resources trying to make this place paradise. The spirit of the age incites us to use excessive resources to create heaven on earth. Jesus says wait for that, and use your resources to bring the message of eternal life to people all over the globe. Instead, dwell on the cost of glory. Glory was quite expensive to open up to us. It cost the Father His Son, and it cost the Son unspeakable suffering and torment. The cost of heaven is measured at the cross.

Beneath the cross, we receive light, which transforms the way we see things. In its light, we can love the unlovely, sacrifice to the undeserving, see broken people as made for glory, obey God when it hurts, and view our troubles as *momentary, light, afflictions, compared to an eternal weight of glory.* (2 Cor. 4:17)

⁵Therefore consider the members of your earthly body as dead to immorality, impurity, passion, evil desire and greed, which amounts to idolatry. ⁶For it is on account of these things that the wrath of God will come, ⁷and in them you also once walked, when you were living in them. ⁸But now you also, put them all aside: anger, wrath, malice, slander, and abusive speech from your mouth. ⁹Do not lie to one another, since you laid aside the old self with its evil practices, ¹⁰and have put on the new self who is being renewed to a true knowledge according to the One who created him—¹¹a renewal in which there is no distinction between Greek and Jew, circumcised and uncircumcised, barbarian, Scythian, slave and freeman, but Christ is all and in all.

Colossians 3:5-11

The Heart-Killing Sin

"If you are at peace with God you are at war with sin."

Let's begin with two questions. Did you wake up this morning at war? If you were in the midst of a war, would you want to know? Surely, there is nothing more tragic or perilous than someone caught in the crossfire of a battle, who doesn't know it! God wants you to know this: If you woke up this morning a believer in Jesus Christ, you woke up at war.

All those who belong to Jesus by faith are at war. If you didn't wake up today with some acknowledgement of being at war, you should have. That's the only way to survive a war. The Bible teaches that when your faith unites you to Christ, you automatically have new relationships. You have *allies:* you are at peace with God and you belong to other believers. You have *adversaries:* you are in conflict with the world, the devil and the flesh (sin). Our focus in this chapter is our adversary, the enemy within, indwelling sin.

Whether or not you acknowledge it, you wake up every day at war with sin because sin is at war with you! This is one of the fundamental facts of the Christian life. It's not to scare you, but to sober and help you. Either you are at peace with sin and at war with God; or you are at peace with God and at war with sin. This text is your call to arms.

Should such militant language surprise us? Not at all! We find sin personified right at the beginning of the Bible. God said to Cain in Genesis 4:7, *"If you do well, will not your countenance be lifted up? And if you do not do well, sin is crouching at the door, and its desire is for you, but you must master it."* In one respect, that is the issue that frames the rest of the story: how will fallen creatures master sin?

There are three elements to understand in order to win the conflict. Using Col. 3:5-11, we understand how Paul frames the war, we understand the method of fighting and we understand the incentives to fighting.

Understand how Paul frames the war.

Therefore... (v. 5) Do you know the implied meaning of *therefore*? It is a war you will win! Aren't there at least three types of wars people fight? A war you know you won't win. A war you don't know you will win. A war you know you will win. In the OT when God says to Israel, go fight this battle, I'll go before you, I will give you the victory—the outcome is certain. Your conflict with indwelling sin is that kind of war. You will eventually win it. Why? God says so, and He won't allow you to lose it.

When God chooses teams, first, He picks losers, but then He makes them winners. Believers ultimately triumph over sin because of their union with Christ. That's why the whole discussion of conflict with sin is framed at the front end by *therefore*. *Therefore* pulls into the discussion verses 1 through 4 where Paul articulates the indicative, who you are, and what God has decisively done for you in Christ. Once he sets forth the indicative, then and only then, does Paul tell you how to live. The indicative is *"you have died"* (v. 1) with Christ and have been *"raised up with Christ."* (v. 1) *"Therefore ... put to death"* sin. This is the difference between religion and Christianity. Religion says, "Do the right stuff and then God accepts you." Christianity teaches, "God accepts you because of your faith, now live as one unconditionally accepted by God."

Victory is certain over sin because those who belong to Christ *already* benefit from His victory over sin and death and Satan, even though they have *not yet* fully received the full, final, complete spoils of His warfare. We benefit *now* from the imputation of our sin to Jesus and His righteousness to us because we have been set free from the tyranny or enslavement of sin. John Murray of Westminster Seminary called this *definitive sanctification*. Since you've been raised up with Christ, the power of sin has been decisively broken in you; no longer is sin a taskmaster you have to obey, although it remains in you, and is still very forceful. Nonetheless, sin is a terrorist without warrant for what it does. But not *until* this earthly life is completed will we be finally and totally freed from the presence of sin. Until that day, we war against the flesh, the impulses of indwelling sin, as a constant way of life.

The other piece of the frame is in verse 9 and 10. To understand the full logic of killing sin, we need read into verse 9 and 10 where Paul further explains the implications of union with Christ. *"You have put off the old self"* (v. 9 ESV), who you were as Adam's prodigy—a rebel against God—and *"have put on the new self"* (v. 10)—notice this—*"which is being renewed in knowledge after its creator."* (v. 10 ESV) Jesus saved you and will make you like Himself. That is a renewal, an ongoing process, by His Spirit, so that gradually you bear the beautiful image of Jesus. Heaven's greatest glory, in other words, the Son of God, the true humanity, gets into you. What does God want to do with your life? Make you like Jesus in moral beauty. That's the reason for killing sin. Sin is contrary to the character of Jesus. It always makes people ugly. Sin dehumanizes you.

We understand this as parents. When our kids begin to hang out with peers whose values are diametrically opposed to our own, we see the effect and naturally grow very concerned. This is Paul's version of WWJD—*What Would Jesus Do*. It isn't so much what would He do, although sometimes that is a helpful question to ask. Rather, is *my* thinking, *my* desires, *my* heart like Christ's and leading me to Christ? In light of God's goal for you—renewal according to the image of Jesus—these sins listed are…ugly. They are *earthly*, contrary to the heavenly pattern or glory. You'll never find them in Jesus. They are contrary to everything Jesus is. They tarnish the beauty of Christ. They poison the heart in which the Holy Spirit dwells.

Understand the method of fighting.

Put to death (v. 5 ESV) … If you think of yourself as a Christian, you must think of yourself as a killer. Either you kill sin or it kills you. What is the big deal? Why is Paul so harsh? Consider a few reasons.

He has unfinished business from Colossians 2, where he boldly asserts, *"rules and regulations have no value in stopping the indulgence of the flesh."* (2:23 ESV) But, he does not want to be misconstrued as saying, live any way you want. Paul never teaches, "Now that you're saved, live for yourself." "Kill sin" draws out the consequences of 3:1-2. When you set your mind on the things above, on Christ, you will begin to see your heart more clearly and you will desire to kill what harms your soul and your Savior.

Paul doesn't want Christians to be surprised. In verse 3, he says *you died with Christ;* a new person has been generated in you by the Spirit. So why, you begin to wonder, do I still sin? The answer is critical to healthy spirituality. Even though the old man you were in Adam has died, all the habits, characteristics, and thought patterns remain. They don't simply go poof—fly away—once you are born again. They are still very much with you and still want to be expressed! Paul explains in Romans 7 that once you are born again, sin springs to life. Sin is at war with you; you must kill it, or it will kill you. What does the text say we should kill? Paul gives a general label: *what is earthly in you.* (Col. 3:5 ESV) *"Earthly"* is opposed to heavenly, where verse 2 exhorts us to fix our minds. *"Earthly"* is a way of life and thinking, which rejects heaven's glory, standards, holiness and King. Consider the two lists. First, verse 5 identifies sins that are sexual in nature: sexual immorality (*porneia*—Greek, meaning any sex apart from monogamous marriage); impurity (sexual sin, the idea is contamination); passion (lust, uncontrolled sexual urges); evil desire (excessive desire to use others as objects for personal satisfaction); covetousness (unchecked, insatiable hunger for selfish, physical pleasure).

Notice the Bible doesn't gloss over sin with tempered euphemisms; sin is labeled. Is Paul just a prude with old-fashioned, repressive hang-ups with sex? Quite the contrary. Paul can't help but drive deep to the core issue. When Paul thinks about sex, he doesn't think in terms of radical individualism and moral neutrality—"I have a right over my own body." Rather, he thinks in terms of the Creator-creature distinction. He looks first at the big picture. We owe God everything, particularly conformity to the principles by which God designed humanity to function. Any failure to serve the Creator or conform to His standards is idolatry. Sexual perversion amounts to idolatry. Narrowly, *idolatry* in verse 5 modifies *covetousness.* By calling it *idolatry,* Paul makes *covetousness,* and all the other sins—by extension—sins of the heart, namely, a heart bent on worshipping a false god. Idolatry is taking a good thing, a good desire, and making it a *must have* thing, the supreme desire. When you seek to repent of any of these sins, you find, at the core, a rejection of God Himself. Coveting essentially believes God isn't enough, because I desire more than God gives me. At the root is dissatisfaction with God Himself. Sexual sin can carry the attitude "you may have created and designed sex for a monogamous relationship, but I refuse to comply with your standards because I know better than you what I need." At heart, this is a slam on the goodness and wisdom of God.

Idolatry is finding life in something—it may be a good thing, sex certainly is—and making it your *only* thing. Idolatry is getting life from something other than God. One sure test of an idol is, if you lost what is in your life, would that make you want to die? Whatever that is, is the source of your real worship. If it's power, control, pleasure, leisure, health, approval—you've put into its hands the power of life and death over you.

Another test is to look at your strongest emotions. They pop up in the second ugly list (v. 8): anger (chronic, steady seething); wrath (flare up, outburst); malice (vicious intent to harm); slander (belittling, harming reputation); obscene talk (that which contaminates listener and speaker); lying (from v. 9—withholding the truth).

What are these? Sins expressed on the tongue, directed at others, revealing a heart of pride and self-absorption, a faithless reaction to people and situations that divides and alienates. Typically, they are sins of a heart that feels threatened. They are sins championed by little rebel terrorists inside you who promote the kingdom of yourself. "I am God and I must have things my way." Paul says, "Strip them off as if they were contaminated clothes." In Belize one summer on a missions trip we worked long and hard pouring cement—a whole lot of it—in the scorching July heat. I deliberately wore a long sleeve shirt to protect my body. At the day's conclusion, I stripped off the shirt and threw it away, for it was drenched with dirt, grime, sweat and cement. After a cleansing, refreshing shower, it would be utterly unthinkable to put it back on. That's Paul's logic here. Having put on Christ, and put off the old man, why would you go after those filthy, grimy garments of lying, slander, anger, etc.?

Sounds easier to do than it is, right? The battle is won in preparation—in prayer. Begin the day asking the Spirit to sap the life from these sins. Romans 8:13 counsels, *"If by the Spirit you are putting to death the deeds of the flesh, you will live."* This work of killing sin is too difficult for you; it can only be accomplished by the Spirit. He is jealous to do it, too.

Ask the Spirit first to minister to you the love of Christ, to sense the goodness of the Lord, so that it becomes increasingly unthinkable to sin against one who loves you so deeply. May the Spirit minister Christ to you—minister who He is in His glory. Col. 3:11 says *"Christ is all, and in all."* He is all that matters, and in all who know Him. Jesus must be more desirable than sin.

If you have a thousand dollar bill, what's your inclination if I ask for it? To pull it back. You want it; it does something for you. But if I asked for it in exchange for a million dollar bill, you'd most gladly give it up for something more desirable. So ask the Spirit to convince you of sin's ugly, harmful nature. You wouldn't naturally seek to hurt yourself. Then ask the Spirit to kill it in you, and to replace it with the virtues of Christ—for lying, truth telling; for slander, blessing; for malice, compassion. While I was golfing one time, a person rode by on a bike and, for no apparent reason, starting taunting me. My first reaction was to run over and tell him off. The Spirit's counsel instead is to bless and curse not.

Understand the incentive to fighting.

Paul mentions two. First, in case we have become so dull by a culture that defines deviance down, Paul sets forth the cosmos in its truest form. *"On account of these things the wrath of God is coming."* (Col. 3:6) That's a worldview statement. For folks who make moral judgments without reference to God, it is a sober corrective. Paul is saying, "Never think of any issue apart from a view to the final judgment." Everyone is accountable for what he or she does. There is justice in the universe; God will see to it. The wrath of God is not a popular concept, understandably so. We naturally don't want to face it, because in our heart of hearts we all know we deserve it. Like death, it is better just shoved to the back of our minds. Paul warns against that. The wrath of God is not shameful. It is never capricious or vindictive, but always just, measured, and righteous. It is God's holy reaction to sin, which ultimately opposes God. However you view the world, keep in focus the coming judgment of God.

That's a future incentive. He also gives a past one. *You used to live that way.* (v. 7) There's the Church: messed-up idolaters upon whom the mercy of Christ worked to bring them out of the misery, deceit, foolishness and destruction of sin. The incentive is to think about what those sins got you. Paul asks his readers in Romans 6:21, *"Therefore what benefit were you deriving from the things of which you are now ashamed? For the outcome of such things is death."*

Yes, former habits are easy to slip back into—they feel normal. But reflect on them. Does coveting ever satisfy you? Do you have enough? What did impure sexual passion ever do for you except produce more, rendering you its slave? What is the end of your bitterness, but more bitterness and heartburn?

The only Oprah show I happened to watch in the last ten years featured a woman who had undergone every conceivable cosmetic surgery available. Oprah asked her, "Are you satisfied with yourself now?" Her reply? "No." What a parable of the heart! Of course, you'll never be satisfied because your heart is much too large to ever be complete with just these created things. You were made for the presence of God. Thank Him that you're restless without Him, and ask Him to draw you to Himself anew.

Please note: No serious study of the Christian's warfare is complete without some discussion of spiritual warfare, i.e., our conflict with Satan. It is beyond the scope of this study to delve into that subject; hence, I refer you to chapter 17 for a brief treatment of it.

[14]Luke, the beloved physician, sends you his greetings, and also Demas.

Colossians 4:14

A Case Study: Where in the World is Demas?

"The Christian fights sin, and dies fighting."

Where in the world is Demas? Who wants to know? We all should want to know! Demas first appears in the Bible in Colossians 4:14. These are Paul's final greetings. The substance of his letter is finished. Rather than end abruptly, Paul follows the custom of his day by sending along greetings from the folks who accompanied him.

You've done this. While on vacation somewhere, you send a postcard to a friend and at the bottom write, "My wife sends her love." Paul writes, "Demas sends his love," as he closes the letter. Demas appears a second time in the Bible in Philemon 24, still a companion to Paul, and a third and final time in 2 Timothy. 2 Timothy is one of Paul's last epistles, written just prior to his execution. Again, according to his custom, Paul finishes the body of his letter and passes on greetings from those around him. But in 2 Timothy 4:9-10, we read these disheartening words: *"Do your best to come to me. For Demas, in love with this present world, has deserted me and gone to Thessalonica."*

Why Demas went to Thessalonica we don't know—and it doesn't matter. Why Demas deserted Paul, we do know, and it does matter. *He was in love with this present world.* Demas was a real person, who now is in heaven or hell. The first we hear of him, he is a companion of the great Apostle Paul. The last we hear of him he is a companion of this present world, having deserted Paul at a critical time in the Apostle's life. We don't know the final chapter of Demas' life, where in the world he ended. The important question is, *"Where in the world are you?"* Will you finish the race of faith?

When we span the six to eight years between Colossians 4 and 2 Timothy 4, we are clearly and soberly warned: how do you keep from following Demas? How do you keep yourself from the pernicious pull of worldliness? Since we are not given any other information about Demas, we're left to apply other scriptures to this case. Let me set forth four propositions to help you resist the way of Demas.

We're all born with a disposition to worldliness.

Your heart in its natural state cannot help but be drawn to worldliness. We inherited this proclivity from Adam and Eve. You could call it Original Sin. Worldliness is summed up in the serpent's temptation; *you shall be as God* (Genesis 3:5). Worldliness is an attitude, a way of looking at life, which puts me at the center. I will decide by myself, without revelation from God, what is good for me. I will judge based on appearances what I will do with my life. I will be my own king; I will do what's right in my own eyes. That's the heart of worldliness—human autonomy. Rather than live under the good, gracious rule of God, humans give their heart's allegiance to something else. We can't help it. We were created to worship God, to give Him our highest affection. But sin forces God to the perimeter, and seeks to draw its life from something created—perhaps even something good—but makes that thing the best: pleasure, power, position, possessions. The first step to fighting worldliness is to own the natural tendency of your heart to worldliness.

Once we are born again, we don't have to be worldly.

The great miracle of the human experience is the life-giving power of God's Spirit to change us. When you become a believer in Jesus Christ, seeing your sinful state as odious to God as it is eternally dangerous, you accept God's gift of forgiveness and God begins to change you. He gives you new desires. Christianity isn't simply, "I'll live forever when I die."

Happily, you possess not only eternal life but also the power in this life, by the Spirit, to be different. We are no longer slaves to our autonomous passions. Don't give up or give in, therefore, to the strong pull of the flesh to worldliness! It's not like a fatal disease, which, once contracted, will certainly kill you. Jesus Christ is in the business of killing sinful urges in those He loves. He is *for* you. Our strong confidence is that the Spirit will change our desires—so ask Him!

As believers, we drift into worldliness, not fall into it.

Demas didn't wake up one day and spontaneously decide to flee from Paul's side. In all likelihood there was a gradual drift, a series of small decisions, mini steps, none of which *alone* could be considered dangerous, but repeatedly left unchecked, produced a build up of spiritual cholesterol in the heart. *"Take care brethren, lest there should be in any of you an evil, unbelieving heart, in falling away from the living God. But encourage one another day after day, as long as it is still called today, lest any one of you be hardened by the deceitfulness of sin."* (Heb. 3:12-13)

The remaining presence of indwelling sin in the believer's heart, like the air hardening a loaf of bread is relentlessly at work, seeking to harden it, rendering your heart less and less tender to the work of the Spirit. This constant intent in you to sin is seeking to harden you, whether or not you feel it happening. A Christian will fight sin every day, and die fighting. Notice that sin works by deceiving: we hide things from ourselves, including the fact of our hiding things from ourselves! This is especially true when it pertains to thinking we are close to God.

Are you close to God? Many people think (rightly) that it is extremely good and desirable to be close to God. Psalm 73 asserts as much: *"the nearness of my God is my good."* People intuitively know that life is better, trials more bearable, and joys more genuine when we are close to God. It's also something we feel uncomfortable questioning in another's experience. If someone claims to be close to God, well, who am I to question that? But is it possible to *feel* close to God but not actually *be* close to God? Is it possible to be self-deceived about being close to God? Is there a counterfeit closeness to God? What does the Bible say about being close to God?

On the one hand, seen from God's point of view, God is close to all of us. Paul preached (Acts 17:27-28) at the Areopagus in Athens that, *"He is not far from any of us, for in Him we live and move and have our being."* That is because His presence fills the universe, His knowledge is exhaustive: He sees us, knows what we think, we can't hide from Him. God is closer to us than we are to ourselves! David asserted in Psalm 139, *"Thou hast searched me and known me, you understand my thoughts from afar,"* and thus wondered, *"where can I flee from your presence?"* God is close to us, not in friendship, but in His omniscience, sovereignty and omnipresence.

But on the other hand, seen from man's point of view, the Bible says we are all born estranged from God and distant from Him. In Psalm 51:5 David says, *"Behold, I was brought forth in iniquity, and in sin my mother conceived me."* There was iniquity, not in the act of conception, but sin is his condition from conception, as a son of Adam. When Adam and Eve disobeyed God, they died spiritually, with the tragic result that all their posterity is born spiritually dead. *"The wicked are estranged from the womb* (Ps. 58:3)... *you have been called a rebel from birth..."* (Is. 48:8). But, the critical question is, do we know this? Do we sense our distance from God, and are we inclined to do anything about it? The Bible explains that the nature of sin is to deceive us about this fact. Sin moves us from God and then hides from us the fact that it is doing so. *"There is a kind who is pure in his own eyes, yet is not washed from his filthiness."* (Prov. 30:12)

Admitting foolishness. Let's explore this dynamic further. Did you ever get a gadget at Christmas that broke? What did you do? You have to try to find out what's wrong and then fix it. Do you ever think of yourself as a broken gadget? Let's suppose you are a broken gadget... what would the Bible say is wrong with you? Our heart is broken, isn't it? It doesn't work the way God made it to work. What was your heart made for? "To love God and to enjoy Him forever" says Question 1 of the Shorter Catechism. Our hearts were made to be perfectly satisfied with the glorious life of God, to be filled with His love and thrilled with His person. But none of us has a heart like that.

Here's the way Proverbs 19:3 puts this. *"The foolishness of man subverts his way, and his heart rages against the Lord."* Since the verse refers to *"man,"* this is speaking about all people as they are naturally born into this world. It is saying that our hearts do not work right. If your heart were not broken, wouldn't you love God with all your heart, soul, strength and mind, and your neighbor as yourself? Yes, for that is exactly what you were made for. You would constantly seek the Lord as your pure, perfect and complete happiness.

So what does *"foolishness"* mean? It means we think we don't need God, that we are good enough ourselves and can find perfect happiness apart from God. Then where does *rage* fit into all this? It means that at the root of my heart, I am angry with God and therefore I do not want Him in my heart. He's kind of like a burglar at the door—I don't want him in my house. "Stay out!" is our attitude. We think in our heart of hearts that God wants to come in as a burglar and rob us of happiness, when actually He is the only One who can make us truly fulfilled. Our rage is insanity.

Here is something very strange: people just don't see that they feel that way. Hardly anyone would say that he hates God, or that his heart rages against God. So how do we know this is true? The Bible tells us so. Look at another verse. *"The heart is more deceitful than all else and is desperately sick, who can understand it?"* (Jer. 17:9) What does it mean that it is *desperately sick*? Simply, that the heart's condition is such that it cannot heal itself. In fact, the heart doesn't even know what the true problem is (that it *rages against the Lord*). How does this *deception* work in the heart? Sin is like a magician. Magicians use at least two kinds of deception for their tricks:

sometimes they hide something that is really there (making you think it is *not* there), and sometimes they make you think something is there that really does not exist (making you think it *is* there). That's exactly what sin does in the heart.

First, sin deceives the heart into thinking that moral goodness is there, that you're sufficient on your own. *"There is a way which seems right to a man, but in the end it is the way of death."* (Prov. 14:12) *"Every man's way is right in his own eyes..."* (Prov. 21:2) This is the foolishness we saw earlier. We think we are good enough without God. We might call this "phantom righteousness."

Second, sin deceives the heart by hiding what really is there, our raging against God. We ought to be raging against sin, but instead we rage against the Lord and concoct in our minds a record of moral goodness.

How do we ever see our hearts as they really are? God has to tell us. The Holy Spirit has to reveal this to us. He is glad to do so, showing us that our hearts are truly self-satisfied (we want our desires not God's), cold (we're sluggish to move toward God) and proud (we think we're pretty good without any outside help).

Now, what is the evidence your heart is like this? Look at your behavior. Why don't you thank God more often? Why don't you love to praise Him? Why aren't you eager to learn the Bible? Why do you fight with other people? Why don't you like to share your possessions? Why aren't you eager to serve the needs of those around you? Why don't you obey God when it hurts? The simple answer is, your heart doesn't work right and you often don't even want to admit it! We make excuses, defend ourselves, bend the rules, feel self-righteous when we do a good thing, and criticize others to make ourselves feel better. But all that just hides the truth that our hearts are empty. God, the One we were made for, is missing! So we try to fill the emptiness with things. Kids do it with games and toys, which make them happy for a little bit. But sooner or later, they get bored. Adults try to fill their hearts with things money can buy—clothes, jewelry, homes, furniture, cars, vacations, relationships. But none of these can fix a broken heart. Your heart is too big ever to be truly satisfied with anything other than the One who made it.

There is hope for hearts that don't work. It is Jesus. He alone can fix the heart. When you see your heart, and the mess it really is, then look right at Jesus. He died to pay for your guilt. His death on the cross is God's guarantee that He is committed to your welfare. In Jesus, we receive the grace of God. We do not get what we deserve (judgment for such raging hearts), but rather receive what we do not deserve (His loving favor and kindness). God doesn't ask us to be good so He will accept us; He accepts us so we can be good. We need Christ's grace for everything!

When you sin, ask for the grace of forgiveness. When you obey, thank Him for the grace He gives. When you need help, ask Him for the grace. When you see the need to change, ask Jesus to change your heart. The Spirit creates a new heart within us. Jesus will show you your sin; ask Him to show you how much better He is than anything else is. Yes, we are broken gadgets. Only the manufacturer knows how to fix us, and only He can! His gospel is enough! Though He sees my raging heart, He loves me still! The One who knows me best loves me most!

Forms of self-deceit. Let's take this notion of sin deceiving us yet another step. How many forms of self-deceit about God might there be? Consider at least two: some are far from God but think otherwise; others are far from God and don't care to do anything about the danger.

How can you tell if you are far from God? One place to attempt to answer the question is Psalm 32. David wrote Psalm 32 as a reflection on one of the greatest periods of self-deception in his life. David sinned grievously against the Lord in a series of lies, murder, adultery and political corruption. Interestingly, it wasn't until the prophet Nathan confronted him in a direct way (2 Samuel 12:1-7; see chapter 5 for the storyline) that he owned the severity of these sins. Apparently, he lived in denial for some time. He must have been self-deceived about the gravity of the whole situation.

How does Psalm 32 help us test whether we are far from God or not?

> Examine your voice of conscience. *"When I kept silent about my sin, my body wasted away through my groaning all day long."* (v. 3) Is something nagging at your conscience, perhaps showing up in a physical manifestation?

> Examine your sorrows. *"Many are the sorrows of the wicked, but he who trusts in the Lord, lovingkindness will surround him."* (v. 10) Often what gets us down is the loss of something we think we need to be whole.

> Examine your counselors. *"I will instruct you and teach you in the way you should go; I will counsel you with my eye upon you."* (v. 8) Who is telling you what is good for you? Where are you getting advice for how to cope?

> Examine the objects of your gladness and delight. *"Be glad in the Lord and rejoice you righteous ones, and shout for joy all you who are upright in heart."* (v. 11) Are the things that make us happy moving us toward or away from intimacy with God?

> Examine your hiding place. *"Thou art my hiding place; thou dost preserve me from trouble; thou dost surround me with songs of deliverance."* (v. 7) What shelter do you seek to feel better about yourself when you disappoint yourself?

Don't hide under the banner of forgetfulness, somehow hoping that if you ignore this, it will go away. Don't hide under the pretense of a false God: "He doesn't see; He doesn't mark sin; He thinks boys will be boys, and grades on a curve; His job is to forgive; my good works will outweigh the bad stuff; God understands me; if I'm sincere, that's enough." What are you trusting to vindicate you in judgment? There is only one advocate with the Father, Jesus Christ the righteous. (1 John 2:1-2) He will plead the merits of His life and blood on your behalf if you trust Him in faith and repentance.

Recognizing the Drift into Worldliness. Now let's return to the notion that sin drifts toward worldliness. How do you recognize that's happening? First, you become less and less hungry for the things of God. Or, seen from another perspective, you become more and more content without the means of grace. So, for example, Hebrews 10:24-25 says, *"Let us consider how to stimulate one another to love and good deeds, not forsaking our own assembling together, as is the habit of some, but encouraging one another, and all the more, as you see the day drawing near."* Here were people who decided they didn't need the local church so they stopped going. "I can be a Christian without going to church!" If you think it's important to look good spiritually, then, you learn to fake it. Demas stayed by Paul's side looking very spiritual, for a season. You can talk the talk, but you know in your heart that you're missing the reality of God's love.

Be honest: we all know what we really desire, what our strongest affections are. You know whether or not you desire to pray and praise (worship), to hear God in His word (preaching), to hear what God is doing in the lives of other believers (fellowship). You know very well whether those things are important to you. You know what you love, what you find attractive. You know for what you yearn, to what you are drawn, to what you give allegiance. You know if your fundamental approach to life is to have as little of God as it takes to get by. Do you know when you are hiding behind your religion in order to look good or merely to feel good about yourself?

Notice that Demas *loved this present world.* At some point, perhaps as gradual as a battleship changing direction, his allegiance changed. He loved this world and its temporary pleasures, rather than the world to come, rather than the world in which Jesus is the heart's greatest delight. At various points, Demas stopped fighting sin and allowed his passions for good things to become inordinate. *"But each one is tempted when he is carried away and enticed by his own lust. Then when lust has conceived, it gives birth to sin; and when sin is accomplished, it brings forth death. Do not be deceived, my brethren. Every good thing bestowed and every perfect gift is from above, coming down from the Father of lights..."* (James 1:14-17) It's significant how James moves from warning about lusts (inordinate desire for good things) to acknowledging God as the source of all good things. What is the connection between the two? There is a huge danger with being satisfied by good things.

The danger of self-satisfaction

How many times have you purchased an appliance, torn into the box, and started using it immediately. You didn't even read all those safety precautions. No, we typically don't do that; we know how it works! And doesn't it usually depend on how powerful the tool is? No one needs safety warnings with an electric razor, but would you want to read the warnings provided with a chainsaw? Yes! Look how much more powerful the chainsaw is! The more powerful the tool, the greater is the risk of danger. Here's the point: I don't know anyone who doesn't gladly receive God's material blessings. But how many of us read the safety warnings that come with them? It is true; every material thing you own is a blessing from God. *"But you shall remember the Lord your God, for it is He who is giving you power to make wealth..."* (Deut. 8:18) *"It is the blessing of the Lord that makes rich, and He adds no sorrow to it."* (Prov. 10:22) Did you know, however, that God provides safety warnings with these blessings?

What is the safety warning given with wealth? We can sum it up in one simple phrase: satisfied hearts are most easily deceived. When God primed Israel in the wilderness for their imminent possession of the Promised Land, He warned them:

"Then it shall come about when the Lord your God brings you into the land which He swore to your fathers, Abraham, Isaac and Jacob, to give you, great and splendid cities which you did not build, and houses full of good things which you did not fill, and hewn cisterns which you did not dig, vineyards and olive trees which you did not plant, and you shall eat and be satisfied, *then watch yourself, lest you forget who brought you from the land of Egypt, out of the house of slavery. You shall fear only the Lord your God; and you shall worship Him and swear by His name."* (Deut. 6:10-13)

"For the Lord your God is bringing you into a good land...a land where you shall eat without scarcity, in which you shall not lack anything...when you have eaten and are satisfied, *you shall bless the Lord your God for the good land which He has given you. Beware lest you forget the Lord your God by not keeping His commandments and His ordinances and His statutes which I am commanding you today; lest, when you have* eaten and are satisfied, *and have built good houses and lived in them, and when your herds and flocks multiply, your silver and gold multiply, and all that you have multiplies, then your heart becomes proud, and you forget the Lord your God who brought you out from the land of Egypt, out of the house of slavery."* (Deut. 8:7-14)

"And I will give grass in your fields for your cattle, and you shall eat and be satisfied. *Beware lest your hearts be deceived and you turn away and serve other gods and worship them."* (Deut. 11:15-16)

Satisfaction breeds self-confidence and forgetfulness. We think we don't need anything else, forget God and therefore, we can be our own interpreters of life. Thus, we will do whatever suits us. *"There also you and your households shall eat before the Lord your God, and rejoice in all your undertakings in which the Lord your God has blessed you. You shall not do at all what we are doing here today, every man doing whatever is right in his own eyes..."* (Deut. 12:7-8) Proverbs 18:11 warns in this regard, *"A rich man's wealth is his strong city, and like a high wall in his own imagination."*

Jesus told a parable of a self-satisfied man who became so consumed with his wealth that he gave no thought to the eternal destiny of his soul (Luke 12:13f; also see Chapter 23). Jesus warned a rich young ruler, apparently unable to part with his wealth for the kingdom of God, *"how difficult it is for a rich man to enter into heaven..."* Paul warned in this vein, *"For we have brought nothing into this world, so we can not take anything out of it either...But those who want to get rich fall into temptation and a snare and many foolish and harmful desires which plunge men into ruin and destruction. For the love of money is a root of all sorts of evil, and some by longing for it have wandered away from the faith, and have pierced themselves with many a pang."* (1 Tim. 6:7-10)

God's agenda in His goodness

Why does God take the risk with wealth? One might say that God is foolish to risk giving us so much, since He knows full well the power of *"satisfaction"* to lure us away from delight and dependence upon Him. Why not keep everyone in the middle class or just above the poverty line, far from the temptation? Why not assign everyone what Agur asked for, *"Two things I have asked of Thee, do not refuse me before I die: keep deception and lies far from me, give me neither poverty nor riches; feed me with the food that is my portion, lest I be full and deny Thee and say, 'Who is the Lord?' Or lest I be in want and steal and profane the name of my God."* (Prov. 30:7-9) What could God's agenda be? Here are some possibilities.

God desires to reveal to us His heart. He is extravagant in blessings because He is so good. *"How great is Thy goodness which Thou hast stored up for those who fear Thee."* (Ps. 31:19)

148

"It is the blessing of the Lord which makes rich." (Prov. 10:22)
"He satisfies your years with good things." (Ps. 103:5)

God allows us wealth so we can see what is in our hearts. Riches are a test, in other words. *"In the wilderness He fed you manna which your fathers did not know, that He might humble you and that He might test you, to do good for you in the end. Otherwise, you may say in your heart, 'My power and the strength of my hand made me this wealth.'"* (Deut. 8:16-17) God is always jealous to show His people that they are sinful and weak and need a savior. He constantly reminded Israel that He saved them in spite of them! (Deut. 7:6-8; 9:4-7) God desires to expose our false loves, and wealth gets to the point very quickly. Will we learn to love God more than things? (Deut. 11:13) Will we learn that obedience is better for us than things? (Deut. 10:12,13; 6:24) Will we learn that only in obedience, and not in wealth alone, will we apprehend the glory of God? (Deut. 10:14,17,21,22)

God satisfies us with good things because they picture the prospect of being satisfied with spiritual wealth in our souls. *"For He has satisfied the thirsty soul, and the hungry soul He has satisfied with what is good."* (Ps. 107:9)

God teaches us the only way to safeguard spiritual health in the midst of prosperity: remember that God saved you (Deut. 15:15, 16:12); rejoice in His presence (Deut. 14:22-26; 16:12,15); and regard those near to His heart—the poor and needy (Deut. 15:7).

Mick Jagger lamented in his smash hit, "I can't get no satisfaction." That may have been a greater blessing than he recognized. When this world's things don't fulfill us, God's mercy drives us to the only reality that can—His presence. Jesus put it in terms of *masters* because the heart will obey one master. *"No one can serve two masters; for either he will hate the one and love the other, or he will hold to one and despise the other. You cannot serve God and mammon."* (Matt. 6:24) No doubt for a season Demas sought to serve both; he flirted with temptation. He wanted human autonomy and God's rule to coexist, just to get along happily. In such dual service, our thinking gets clouded. In fact, we could say at one level the reason Demas loved this present world is he stopped thinking. Jesus said, *"For what will a man be profitted, if he gains the whole world, and forfeits his soul? Or what will a man give in exchange for his soul?"* (Matt. 16:26) And he stopped thinking because he stopped loving Jesus.

Worldliness results from guarding the heart.

Everyone guards his heart, in one form or another. There is a guarding which preserves life and there is a guarding which destroys it. The kind of guarding which destroys life is depicted in Prov. 1:7. *"Fools despise wisdom and instruction..."* If you want to be very susceptible to worldliness, keep others out. Sin will have a man when he is alone. Tell yourself that no one can tell you what's best for you. No one needs to know your weaknesses. When the auditors ask questions, lie to them.

A subtle variation on keeping others out of your heart is spending time only with people within your economic class. Typically, wealthy folks socialize with other wealthy people, who are highly unlikely to challenge each other about the morality of their spending habits. In contrast, if people of significant means spent time with much poorer Christians their values would have to change.

The kind of guarding which preserves life is depicted in Prov. 4:23, the theme verse for this book. *"Watch over your heart with all diligence, for from it flow the springs of life."* The image is powerful. In ancient times, all life depended upon water. Your spring was indispensable to your survival. The proverb challenges you to view your heart as a spring, as water is vital to your physical existence, so your heart is vital to your spiritual existence. Never let anyone poison the spring. Never let anything poison the heart. Demas let the pollutants of materialism poison his heart. Had he read Paul's admonition,

"No longer be conformed to this world, but be transformed by the renewing of your mind"? (Romans 12:2) J.B. Phillips' translation says, "Don't let the world squeeze you into its own mold." The world put its squeeze on Demas. What are you doing to keep from being assimilated into this world's values? *"Watch over the heart with all diligence, for from it flow the springs of life."*

[18]If the world hates you, you know that it has hated Me before it hated you. [19]If you were of the world, the world would love its own; but because you are not of the world, but I chose you out of the world, therefore the world hates you. [20]Remember the word I said to you, "A slave is not greater than his master." If they persecuted Me, they will also persecute you; if they kept My word, they will keep yours also. [21]But all these things they will do to you for My name's sake, because they do not know the One who sent Me. [22]If I had not come and spoken to them, they would not have sin, but now they have no excuse for their sin. [23]He who hates Me hates My Father also. [24]If I had not done among them the works which no one else did, they would not have sin; but now they both have seen and hated Me and My Father as well. [25]But they have done this in order that the word may be fulfilled that is written in their law, "They hated Me without cause." [26]When the Helper comes, whom I will send to you from the Father, that is, the Spirit of truth, who proceeds from the Father, He will bear witness of Me, [27]and you will bear witness also, because you have been with Me from the beginning.

John 15:18-27

Are You Armed for the Conflict?

"God never leaves us defenseless for the conflicts He's called us to fight."

How often have you seen something like this in the movies. A man has to leave his bride all alone in a potentially threatening situation. So he gives her these instructions: "Stay here, lock the door, if I'm not back in three hours, call the Cavalry." And then in that last dramatic moment, puts a gun in her hand, "If you need it, use it." *He leaves, satisfied that his bride, though alone, is armed for potential trouble.*

Jesus also left His disciples in a world of potential trouble. What encouragement does He give His downcast followers? Is He satisfied that His bride is sufficiently armed for its inevitable conflict with the world? Apparently so. How, then, has He armed us? In three ways. Jesus has well fortified His bride in her conflict with the world by providing our love for one another, the wisdom of Jesus' word and the ministry of the Holy Spirit.

Our love for one another

We'll miss some of our critical fortification if we overlook John 15:12. *"This is My commandment, that you love one another."* This may seem obvious to many of you, but in our age of individualism and escapisms (computers, internet, videos), I suspect we are not as quick to take advantage of this resource as we should be.

How encouraging to our hearts to be loved by others in the body of Christ, especially when the world hates us. When the world persecutes you, the saints should edify you, bandage your wounds, care for your needs, weep with you, stand beside you and help bear your burdens. William Gurnall said, "The chains of love are stronger than the chains of fear."

Conversely, how it breaks the heart of Jesus when we treat each other the way we expect the world to treat us! We can understand why *they* do, but how is it *we* can hate one for whom Christ died? The world in darkness cannot distinguish a religious person from a Christ follower... *except* by the one God-ordained means to catch their eye. *"By this all men will know that you are My disciples, if you love one another."* (John 13:35) Pray constantly for God to use you to be a blessing in the lives of your brothers and sisters as they slug it out with the world, the flesh and the devil. Don't forget, if you seem to be doing better than someone else, isn't it because you've been *given* more grace than they have?

The wisdom of Jesus' word

Jesus' word provides an in-depth explanation of *the nature of the world's conflict with the believer*, so that when we experience it, we won't panic but will respond in grace. To keep us from feeling like this is a personal attack, Jesus sets forth a simple paradigm describing the inevitable nature of the conflict: the world hates *God*, the world therefore hates *God's Son* and the world necessarily hates *those who identify with the Son*. Let me illustrate this.

Years ago, a neighbor's dog tried to attack my dog. The problem was, my dog was inside my house and the other dog was outside. So their dog broke a pane in the living room window in its attempt to attack my dog! When I went down the street to inform the neighbor about the situation and to ask for help replacing the window, the first thing she blurted out was, "Oh you Christians!" Now to this day I'm not sure I understand the connection between her dog's antics and my faith. But one thing was clear; I was somehow guilty by association. I think she had some issues with Christians, and I represented yet another problem for her…somehow! So should I be defensive? Did she really have a beef with me? Should I be angry with God for experiencing her misplaced wrath? Should I give up the faith because it will often render me so misunderstood in the world?

What's the point? I should be understanding and patient with her. If her heart is at war with God and she has struggles with Christians, and she knows I'm a Christian, I should *expect* her to lash out at me.

Why should we be patient while suffering at the hands of the world? Because the world has been in darkness for a long time and the kingdom of Christ will, humanly speaking, take a long time to overcome it. But since God is sovereign, *"working all things according to the counsel of His own will"* (Eph. 1:11), nothing can thwart His purposes. If He has ordained these sufferings and setbacks, we can wait on God, even when we don't understand why things happen as they do. That is a sure mark of faith: *trust without all the answers*. The persecuted apostles demonstrated this trust in God's sovereignty by praying. *"For truly in this city there were gathered together against Thy holy servant Jesus, whom Thou didst anoint, Herod, Pilate, along with the Gentiles and the peoples of Israel, to do whatever Thy hand and Thy purpose predestined to occur.. And now, Lord, take note of their threats, and grant that Thy bondservants may speak Thy word with all confidence…"* (Acts 4:27-29)

Jesus' word gives wisdom to understand our *calling in the conflict*. We will stumble (John 16:1) unless we understand our relationship to the world. Historically, the church errs in two opposite directions.

On the one hand, the church accommodates to the world. It is too much like the world. According to John 15:19, the Church is to be *"in the world but not of the world."* Jesus would later say, *"I do not ask the Father to take them out of the world, but to keep them from the evil one. "* (John 17:15) In other words, "Father, take the world out of them!"

If the church's agenda differs so little from the world's, of course the world will have no conflict with it! Sadly, the battle cry of organizations like the World Council of Churches has been "the world must set the agenda for the church." I hope you see that is totally backwards! Such a Church proves to be as irrelevant as it is impotent. The social gospel approach of last century featured "a God without wrath who brought a people without sin into a kingdom without judgment by a Christ without a cross."

The cross *is* the stumbling block without which the world will never change. It is the centerpiece of the Church's agenda, such that Paul could remind the Corinthians, *"I determined to know nothing among you except Jesus Christ, and Him crucified."* (1 Cor. 2:2) Beloved, if there is nothing about you that stands out in our culture, you need to re-examine your core values, commitments and priorities. Jesus warned, *"Woe to you when all men speak well of you!"* It is infinitely better to have the whole world for our enemies and God for our friend, than to have the whole world for our friends and God for our enemy. Whoever marries the spirit of this age finds himself a widower in the next. *"What does it profit a man to gain the whole world and forfeit his soul?"* Your great joy and peace will come only as you center on one ultimate concern: What glorifies God?

On the other hand, the church errs by escaping from the world, by retreating, withdrawing and avoiding the world. Where my family goes to the beach, we find lots of fiddler crabs. They live on the beach but you can never catch them. As soon as you glance in their direction, they scurry back into their holes in the sand. Is that how Jesus would have you respond in this world? Certainly, to avoid clear evils and temptations, we must flee immorality. But the Church that retreats from the world will have no transforming impact in it; it can't hate a Christ-lover it can't see! This mentality rightly stresses that we should not be *of* the world (*"he who is a friend of the world makes himself an enemy of God"* (James 4:4)), but forgets that Christ has left us in culture to redeem it.

If the first error is the salt losing its saltiness (Matt. 5:13), this error is hiding your light under a basket (Matt. 5:15). God calls us to fulfill the cultural mandate, set forth in the Garden of Eden, to subdue the whole earth. The time is long overdue to send believers into all spheres of life—journalism, the arts, science, industry, medicine, education. The world will seek to marginalize clear-thinking Bible believers, but let them admire our pursuit of excellence.

Do you see that both errors share the same problems? Both fail to realize that Christ came to redeem the world, to transform it; it is the theatre of His renewing work of the cosmos. Neither view requires the believer to be dependent on the Lord; only when we feel the rub of being different will we throw ourselves upon the Lord in prayer. Both views deny the power of the gospel.

The ministry of the Holy Spirit

In our struggle to be well armed for trouble, here is the Cavalry. The Holy Spirit is the weapon of weapons, the Help to beat all others. Paul said, *"For though we walk in the flesh, we do not war according to the flesh, for the weapons of our warfare are not of flesh, but divinely powerful for the destruction of fortresses..."* (2 Cor. 10:3-4)

How encouraging that in the middle of this John 15 passage on the world's hatred of believers, Jesus speaks of the Spirit. *"When the Helper comes..."* When the Cavalry comes! For the disciples, the Spirit came at Pentecost with power and glory. Every believer has the Spirit in his salvation package. He is the Helper or *paraclete* (Greek), the One called along side, because He comforts us, strengthens us, is there for us, helps us to pray.

Jesus says, *"I will send Him from the Father"* (John 15:26). The Spirit is the gift of the Son given by the Father to confirm in the hearts of His people that they belong to God. He is sent as the

157

pledge of the Father's love, as the down payment of our eternal inheritance. By the Spirit's indwelling, God is taking of Himself, as it were, depositing Himself in us, with full intent to bring back into Himself all of Himself. If you deposited your inheritance in a variety of places, on that great day you would collect it for your pleasure. So the Father will call us all to Himself as His inheritance on that great day.

Jesus sends the Spirit from the throne of grace where He rules the world. He sits at the right hand of God, governing His entire creation for His own glory, and interceding for the welfare of His people. The Spirit assures us of His rule and draws us in prayer with boldness to the One who accomplishes His will on earth through our prayers. The Spirit says to our hearts, "Grace is yours, mercy is abundant, come and drink of His love until you are satisfied." *"They drink their fill of the abundance of Thy house; and Thou dost give them to drink of the river of Thy delights."* (Psalm 36:8)

He is also *the Spirit of truth* (John 15:26); by the Holy Spirit, we are taught the things of God. He opens our minds, takes the truth of Christ, and teaches, informs, corrects, leads, illumines us with the deposit of truth in the scriptures. Calvin said,

"Here Jesus contrasts the testimony of the Spirit to that of the world. If He supports our conscience, we will never give way. The world will indeed rage against you. Some will mock and others will curse your teaching. But none of their attacks will be so violent as to break the firmness of your faith when the Holy Spirit has been given to you to establish you by His testimony. Indeed, when the world rages on all sides, our one protection is that God's truth, sealed by the Holy Spirit in our hearts, despises all that is in the world. For if it were subject to men's judgments, our faith would be overwhelmed a hundred times a day."

Jesus explains, *"He will bear witness of me"* (v. 26). Many of you decorate your homes for Christmas; no doubt, a few of you place a lovely wreath on the door, and set a spotlight on the ground showcasing the wreath. The spotlight, invisible, exists to highlight the wreath, not itself. In the same way, the Spirit's job is to showcase Jesus, to turn all the light on Jesus. He jealously desires all the glory to go to Jesus, to so highlight Jesus that our faith settles on Him alone.

That is not an end in itself. Notice Jesus adds, *"and you will bear witness also"* (v. 27). The Spirit shines the light on Jesus; He opens our eyes to behold His beauty, and fills our heart with the desire to tell others. The Spirit creates holy gossip. He wants to fill our hearts with wondrous thoughts of Jesus so that we can't help but to speak of Him.

This is how Jesus subverts the agenda of the world in hostility to Him. He puts us on the offensive with the Spirit, so that rather than the world pulling us into its ethos, we are pulling it into the kingdom of grace. In other words, your best defense against worldly hostility is your witness into the world. When you see it happen, you only want to see it more! You begin to know the pleasure of seeing God change world lovers into Christ lovers. When I need encouragement, I remember testimonies of the saints God changed into those who love and live for His Son.

This is also how Jesus subverts our love of the world. When our heart's concentration is on the world's need, the Spirit loosens your affection for the pleasures you think you need. This dynamic is evident in my friend Lisa Brown, a short-term missionary to Ukraine. In emails describing power outages, her apartment being 61 degrees, and minimal food, she wrote, "Despite the inconveniences, I'm overjoyed to be here. The Lord is gradually removing from my heart my American need for immediate satisfaction. I'm realizing there are a lot of things I can do without." When we lay hold of all that Jesus freely gives us for our conflicts, we know He is the one thing without which we can never do!

42Jesus said to them, "If God were your Father, you would love Me...43Why do you not understand what I am saying? It is because you cannot hear My word. 44You are of your father the devil, and you want to do the desires of your father. He was a murderer from the beginning, and does not stand in the truth, because there is no truth in him. When he speaks a lie, he speaks from his own nature; for he is a liar, and the father of lies. 45But because I speak the truth, you do not believe Me."

John 8:42-45

Father of Lies, Son of Truth

"Is what you believe about life really true?"

On one of my many trips flying between Texas and Virginia, I heard those dreaded words from the gate agent, "We have a delay. We are waiting for a mechanic." My first thought was, "It better be the best one you have!" Just minutes later, the same lady announced, "The problem is fixed, we're now ready to board." It seemed a little too fast for my tastes, but what do I know? They usually give passengers very little information about the airline's operations anyway. But it still entered my mind: Was she telling the truth? Did the mechanic fix the problem, or simply lie about it?

No one likes being lied to, especially when your life depends on it at 31,000 feet in the air. We all love and need the truth, at least to some degree. Wouldn't life be treacherous if you never knew when someone was telling you the truth? Don't we all, regardless of religious commitment, crave to be told the truth? Even the most strident defender of moral relativism hates to be lied to! Think of your doctor's evaluation of your condition, or your broker's advice on stocks. Or how would you feel about your mechanic's assessment of a problem with your steering, just before your beloved daughter drives the curviest mountain road in the country. There are endless examples of situations where anyone would crave the truth and not hesitate to call lying absolutely wrong.

Well, are there lies about God, about heaven, and about how to be right with God? Jesus says so in the passage before us. Jesus is saying you need truth about the biggest issue of life: who you are in relation to God, and where you hope to spend eternity. It's one thing for the mechanic to lie about his properly fixing the engine, and then finding yourself dropping out of the sky to your death—and another for you to believe a lie about what happens next, for all eternity.

In John 8:44, Jesus describes the world; He provides a cosmology, a worldview statement. We could sum it up this way: The human experience is captivated by some big lies about man, God and the afterlife. We are lied to about the most important issues in life. Why? Because, as Jesus said to His audience, *"You are of your Father the devil; he is a liar and the father of lies."* Like father, like son. We all know the principle: children are highly influenced by parents. Specifically, what you hear from your father profoundly colors your world. Since the whole world lies under the power of Satan, and since it is his nature to lie, consequently, it is our nature to believe his lies, to be gullible and deceived. Paul explains in 2 Cor. 4:4, *"the god of this world has blinded the minds of the unbelieving, that they might not see the light of the gospel of the glory of Christ, who is the image of God."*

Even the Jews, the last folks on earth I would expect to be clueless about spiritual reality (after all, they are the chosen people, privy to the very oracles of God), suffer from the "living a lie" syndrome. So the whole world, says Jesus, is in darkness; it lies under the power of the evil one, and simply doesn't get it spiritually. That's what Jesus means in John 8:45, *"Because I speak the truth, you do not believe Me,"* a virtual restatement of verse 43, *"Why do you not understand what I am saying? Because you cannot hear My word."* Jesus is revealing that in our heart of hearts we simply refuse to hear the truth about our alienation from God, about our sin and God's righteous judgment.

But thankfully, that's not the end of the story! Jesus has come as the light of the world! He has come to set you free! From the tyranny of ignorance, from the lies of the deceiver, from your slavery to sin, from the condemnation of your guilt, free to be all that God created you to be! Jesus is the revealer of the truth, the faithful prophet of God who brings the word of truth, and who is the living Word. When are you free to drive the treacherous mountain road in the thick of night? Only when you have headlights! We all crave that kind of true direction because it yields the freedom to enjoy life.

Jesus says, "The world is full of lies about spiritual reality that you are bent to embrace. For my part, I'll tell you the truth." What is your part? To constantly ask the question, "What do I believe? Is what I believe about life really true?" How does my understanding square with the word of God?

That means, as Paul stated in 2 Cor. 3, *"we are not ignorant of the schemes of the devil"*, you must continue in your pursuit to master the truth *("if you abide in my word, you will know the truth")*. You must continue to renounce lies you are tempted to believe. Here are a few examples.

Lies about how to be accepted by God

> *Lie:* All God wants is sincere people. But wait. Who is ever really truly sincere and without hypocrisy? And is it not possible to be sincerely wrong? And doesn't everyone require certain standards?

> *Lie:* We can't really figure out God, so just do your best. Well, who is defining best? And what justice is meted out in the end for the real schmucks in the world?

> *Lie:* Keep all the rules and God will let you in to heaven. The Jews to whom Jesus is speaking in John 8 believed that.

These are all lies from the father of lies. They cost people eternity. They originate with the one who hates human beings because they bear God's image, and who is unrelenting in his pursuit of their destruction.

The truth is so much better! We are accepted by God not for any of our efforts! God accepts you in spite of your sin, by His mercy, because He spared not His own Son and delivered Him up to death on the cross for you in your place. Eternal life is a gift God graciously gives to anyone who asks for it by faith.

Lies about what will make you happy

When Jesus says in John 8:44, *"you do the desires of your father,"* He is indicating two truths. One, we all desire some form of happiness, and two, our desires are governed by our father, who in this case is a liar. Put it this way, what do you really desire, and why? Honestly, God's word shows me that I really want to be God, to be king of a little domain where I answer only to myself. (Doesn't that feel good?) The Bible calls this pride, the insatiable thirst in my heart to have my world revolve around me, and if I happen to be religious, to have God serve me. It was for this very desire that Satan fell from his status as an angel in heaven.

One of the greatest lies propagated upon human beings is, you will never be happy being holy. Or, put another way, you will only be happy when you do exactly and only what you want to do. When you are your own boss, setting your own rules for yourself, that's fulfillment. It's as if we have this thing in us that resists accepting the Father's love, and resultantly, loving the Father. We find His commandments restrictive of our desires. We believe the lie that God is boring, unfulfilling and undesirable. Why else would we be ignoring Him?

Jesus says in John 8:42, *"If God were your Father, you would love me."* I could not think of a more profound definition of happiness: God is My Father, I'm loving Jesus. Jesus will only tell me the truth, He will love and protect me, He will most certainly accomplish my best. For an enormous variety of reasons, we simply buy into a lie about that. Here's a little test: when was the last time you were filled up with the love of God and love for Christ? Psalm 43:4 says, *"God is my exceeding joy."*

Lies about what discourages you

Satan loves to slander God. He relishes opportunities to accuse God of being a bad guy, and of being after you to discourage you. The truth is, God is the God of all hope, the God of all encouragement. It is impossible for God to discourage His own. Sometimes my daughter Laura wonders if I'm trying to stack the deck when we play UNO. I explain to her, "I am your father, and I love you, and I want no harm for you, and I would never cheat my children." Take that sentiment and multiply it a billion times, and that is how your heavenly Father feels about you. Though He will discipline us for our good, that we may share His holiness, there's never an ounce of discouragement in Christ for His own. Satan will lie to you about that, but you must pound into your mind the truth about God revealed in Scripture.

What does this text require of you? At least this—that you put on the *full armor of God* described in Eph. 6:10-18 on a regular basis and that you constantly ask Christ for grace to develop a well-disciplined thought life. Paul calls it *"taking every thought captive to the obed-ience of Christ."* (2 Cor. 10:5) *"Whatever is true, honorable, right, pure, lovely, whatever is of good repute, if there is any excellence or anything worthy of praise, let your mind dwell on these things."* (Phil. 4:8) *"Set your mind on the things above, not on the things that are on earth."* (Col. 3:2) *"Do not be conformed to this world, but be transformed by the renewing of your mind..."* (Rom. 12:2)

PART IV

THE HEART AT WORK

¹Hear my prayer, O Lord, give ear to my supplications! Answer me in Thy faithfulness, in Thy righteousness! ²And do not enter into judgment with Thy servant, for in Thy sight no man living is righteous. ³For the enemy has persecuted my soul; he has crushed my life to the ground; he has made me dwell in dark places, like those who have been long dead. ⁴Therefore my spirit is overwhelmed within me; my heart is appalled within me. ⁵I remember the days of old; I meditate on Thy doings; I muse on the work of Thy hands. ⁶I stretch out my hands to Thee; my soul longs for Thee, as a parched land. ⁷Answer me quickly, O Lord, my spirit fails; do not hide Thy face from me, lest I become like those who go down to the pit. ⁸Let me hear Thy lovingkindness in the morning; for I trust in Thee; teach me the way in which I should walk; for to Thee I lift up my soul. ⁹Deliver me, O Lord, from my enemies; I take refuge in Thee. ¹⁰Teach me to do Thy will, for Thou art my God; let Thy good Spirit lead me on level ground. ¹¹For the sake of Thy name, O Lord, revive me. In Thy righteousness bring my soul out of trouble. ¹²And in Thy lovingkindness cut off my enemies, and destroy all those who afflict my soul; for I am Thy servant.

Psalm 143

A Prayer to Start the Day

"God allows us to struggle so He can drive us to Himself."

Most of us have had the opportunity to take a long trip in the family car. Getting the car ready for the road has always been sort of fun for me. I fill the gas tank, change the oil, clean the windows, adjust the tire pressure, clean it inside and out, put in the maps, fill the cubbyholes with snacks and bottled water and so on. When I'm finished, I have this great feeling of completeness, readiness and confidence.

Now, wouldn't that be a fantastic way to start each day? Do you leave the home with that sense of confidence and anticipation? If your days seem to be eating up your sense of life and joy, perhaps it is because you aren't preparing for your day the way God would have you. Maybe He is allowing you to struggle so you can be driven to Him and Him alone, as the giver of grace for each new day.

Psalm 143 helps you understand a pattern for how to pray at the start of each day. You don't always have to pray this way. But present in the psalm are the key elements to preparing for a joyful, Spirit-led day, just as the items I first mentioned are essential for preparing for a long road trip.

You may be wondering if David composed this psalm *specifically* for the start of a day, or on the occasion of a long camel trip. Perhaps neither. Essentially this psalm is a prayer for deliverance and guidance, probably meant for personal and corporate singing. The focus is David's trouble with his enemies.

How could that be relevant for you and me? Well, the longer I live as a Christian, the greater sense I have that daily I'm always potentially in trouble. There's not a day this side of heaven that I wake up and am not at some risk spiritually. So the psalm is always applicable. Most of us struggle to live with strong and abiding encouragement. So, in as much as David is hurting, then the psalm is a help to us, too.

To answer the question then, "How do you pray when you are hurting or when you are at risk spiritually," we can walk right through the text.

Appeal to God's character

Prayer, of course, is offered to God. Therefore, David is quick to remind himself and God just whom he addresses. The first thing David says is, *"Hear my prayer, O Lord."* (v. 1) That tells us one critical factor in prayer: we are in covenant relationship with God. The title "LORD" translates God's covenant name, *Yahweh*. It is the name by which God revealed Himself to Israel. Remember when God answered Moses' request, *"who shall I say is sending me?"* *"Tell them* [Israel, held captive in Egypt] *I AM sent you."* The nations may know Him by one of His other names (such as *Elohim*), but *Yahweh* (I AM who I AM) answers the question, "Who are you God, in relation to us, your people?" Because David understands that, in the covenant, God swears to uphold His people, he freely and unabashedly cries out for God's attention. *Hear me, give ear to me, answer me!* Wouldn't that sound so presumptuous, even audacious, if God is simply the supreme ruler of the universe, and David is arbitrarily demanding an audience for himself? Do you have the right to barge into the office of the President of the United States, or of IBM for that matter, and boldly assert, "Answer me"?

But David knows he belongs to the Lord. He has no hesitation concluding, *"I am your servant."* (v. 2) He knows who he is in relation to *Yahweh* and thus he exercises what Hebrews 3 and 10 calls "confidence," or "bold access." Dear believer, David is no more privileged than you are, if you belong to Christ. Because God has given Himself to us in Christ, not withholding any good thing, we cry out to the Lord in prayer. We don't have to earn our way, nor can we. Do you feel *worthy* of such bold prayer? You are deceiving yourself if you do, unless your worthiness is founded upon Christ alone. Do you feel *unworthy* of such bold prayer? Well you are! But the gospel of grace and mercy declares us welcome to the throne of grace—not for any of our own merits—but through the merits of Christ alone. He has cleansed us for God's holy presence, He has opened the way, He has torn the curtain in two *"once and for all time,"* declares Hebrews 10:14,19-22.

Do you see? If we don't pray, we deny the work of Christ. If we don't pray, we must think we control our destiny, or that we do not need God. No, God is more delighted to hear our bold cries than we can imagine. *O Lord, give ear.* (v. 1) In saying as much, we proclaim God as our provider-King, Christ as our mediator, ourselves as His own possession. John Newton wrote:

Thou art coming to a King
Large petitions with thee bring
For His grace and power are such
None can ever ask too much.

That is one way that David appeals to God's character; He calls Him "Lord, my covenant head." Notice next he pleads, *"answer me in Thy faithfulness, in Thy righteousness."* (v. 1) The natural way we think is, "Answer because I deserve it." David is under no such pretension. He says to God, "Hear me because you are faithful and righteous. Faithful to your people, yes. Faithful to your promises, yes!" Here David expresses confidence in God's goodness, in His word keeping. The faithfulness of God finds its most glorious expression in the sending of His Son, Jesus Christ. David looked forward to that event believing God would keep His promise to send a mediator, while we look back to the cross as the fulfillment of that promise. And he adds, *"in Thy righteousness"* (v. 1). "I am confident you will do what is right, and I won't ask you to violate your own holy will."

If David is consciously aware of these unchangeable attributes in God, then he is equally aware of his own frailty. *"Do not enter* *into judgment with Thy servant, for in Thy sight no man living is righteous."* (v. 2) Spurgeon remarks here, "God's sight is piercing and discriminating; the slightest flaw is seen and judged; and therefore pretense and profession cannot avail where that glance reads all the secrets of the soul."[*] David knows that God sees all, measures all and finds us all severely missing the mark. Paul said as much, *"For all have sinned and fall short of the glory of God."* (Rom. 3:23) Solomon knew it, *"Who can say I have cleansed my heart, I am pure from my sin?"* (Prov. 20:9) Jesus taught man's thorough corruption with uncompromised clarity.

So David's brutal honesty about his heart is as sure a plea for mercy as one could possibly make. If God marks sins, who could stand? (Ps. 130:1) "I am guilty, I know what I deserve." Yet David is, remarkably, unafraid! Why? Because his platform for standing in God's holy presence is not built with the toothpicks of his own good deeds, he stands as a sinner accepted purely by grace. David believes the gospel; God alone justifies unrighteous people through the substitutionary work of His Son.

David models a great way to begin prayer: adoring God for His holiness and mercy, thanking Him for the gospel, falling humbly at Jesus' feet through whom we have received pardon, righteousness, grace, deliverance, life, the promises of God. You woke up at peace with God; nothing will change that. There is nothing to prove or earn. Your Father awaits your cries.

Articulate your complaint

David jumps right into describing his situation to God. *"For the enemy has persecuted my soul; he has crushed my life to the ground; he has made me dwell in dark places, like those who have been long dead."* (Ps. 143:3) Now is that silly, since God already knows? Not at all. David gives the theme, "I feel like I'm in a coffin, buried alive." Then he follows with the result of his enemies' persecution, *"Therefore my spirit is overwhelmed within me; my heart is appalled."* (v. 4) Sometimes you may realize, by

---

[*] Charles Haddon Spurgeon, *The Treasury of David*, Vol.3, p.335

articulating your problem, that you don't have it right. The Spirit may convict you differently. This happened to me as I was complaining to God about someone and the Spirit clearly impressed this truth upon me, "don't worry about how you're being treated, show him the love of Christ."

Other times, articulating your complaint allows you to see how you may be dressing up the coffin. When you are *feeling* buried alive by your tormentors, what do you do? Run to the mall for a "feel good about myself" thing? Visit a web site that leads you into all sorts of self-destructive fantasy? Pump up your sense of worth by knocking someone else down? Jesus cried the same anguish of verse 3, but concluded, *"not My will, but Yours be done."* (Luke 22:42) The same grace that empowered Jesus to stay faithful to the Father is abundantly yours in Christ by the Spirit.

Who are your enemies? How do you pray verse 3, knowing that David had flesh and blood people in view, maybe his own son Absalom, maybe his best friend's dad King Saul? Maybe you really don't have that sort of hostility in your life. You have three enemies that will crush you unless you are vigilant. They are the world, the flesh and the devil. Pray for grace to see through the world's way of thinking, to be protected from the Evil One (from lies, deceptions, accusations), and for the Spirit to keep in check indwelling sin. It is a given that unless you proactively pray against these, they are all too powerful for you. That is what I meant when I began with the assertion that I'm potentially in trouble every day, at risk all the time.

Prayer against these foes will safeguard you wonderfully. God wants you to pray this way because this will show you how much you need to depend on Him, and that's what really releases the Spirit in you. Grace flows downhill; it comes abundantly to those who cry out for it. But you need to pray consistently more than this...

Adjust your focus

In verse 5, David cuts against the modern pragmatic grain. Modern folks look for action plans; David does theological reflection. Look at the verbs in verse 5—*"I remember, meditate, muse…"* What a lesson! David is overwhelmed, so he gets out the books—the book that records God's kind dealings with him in the past (*"days of old"*), the book recording God's acts in providence (*"all Thy doings"*) and the book of creation (*"the works of His hands"*).

Sounds like Psalm 111:3—*"Great are the works of the Lord, they are* studied *by all who delight in them."* David says, "When the flesh, the devil and the world rear their ugly heads to overwhelm me, I put the face of the Lord in front of me. I study His works, character and blessings He has lavished upon me." It's either that, or a pity party, right? Either you magnify the Lord, or despair. Either triumph emotionally in God's sovereignty, or retreat to an unreal world of nostalgia. David does not try to recreate the past by fleeing to a simpler time, nor does he retreat into a stoic "whatever will be, will be." He instead focuses on God's work, on His wisdom and goodness. Now look where such reflection leads David…

Acknowledge your needs

The result of David's work in meditation is a shameless expression of longing for the Lord. *"I stretched out my hands to thee, my soul longs for thee as a parched land."* His hands express his soul; he holds empty hands before the Lord. I have nothing to offer, but I am not condemned (*"I trust in thee."* (Ps. 143:8) A guilty person cowers back.), nor am I satisfied. My spirit fails, don't hide your face, I need to sense your presence; ah yes, this is what my soul needs, *"to hear your lovingkindness in the morning."* (v. 8) David needs revival.

When you wake up tomorrow, there are lots of things you'd like to hear; the air conditioner running, the coffee brewing, your child's sweet voice, your wife's affirmation, your stocks are flying, rain is in the forecast—all great gifts of God! But what you *must* hear, lest any of those good things become *the thing*—an idol, the thing for which you live—you *must* hear Jesus say, "I love you; I will never let you go; I am yours, you are mine; I have put your guilt away!" His is the one voice that can cheer when sorrow stops up the ear. Honestly, do your devices to soothe your sorrows actually work? Do your "pain managers" really address the core issues of your heart and lead you to freedom? What are you hearing in the morning?

The start of a good day is, *"cause me to hear Your love, I trust in You."* I know of no surer place to find that certainty than in the revealed word of God. David is praying for revival. *"For thy name sake, O Lord, revive me; in thy righteousness, bring my soul out of trouble."* (v. 11) You don't have to present your righteousness to God to get His attention. "Revive me Lord, for the glory of your name, for the revelation of your character through me, to display me to a broken world as a trophy of your grace." Can God resist answering that prayer?

The last truth to stress is David's plea for instruction. He says repeatedly, *"teach me, deliver me, teach me to do your will, let thy good Spirit lead me on level ground..."* (v. 8-10) This is the evidence of a revived heart. The goodness of Christ received will produce new longings for obedience and dependence upon the Lord. The self-made man charts his own course. The saved man pleads with the Lord for the way, *"You* are God, *You* know the way, *You* are the path-cutter, *You* alone are wise, lead me!" *Lead me on level ground* (v. 10) for I by myself am prone to stumble, my heart without your Spirit will always gravitate toward self-fulfillment, rather than Spirit-fulfillment. Psalm 119 is a long commentary on how delightful the law of God is to a revived heart.

Do you see the order? Grace plows up the hard ground of the heart so it can receive the seed of the word. Many of us are unaffected by Bible-reading because our hearts are not plowed up by the experience of Jesus' love. Search your heart—are you teachable? If not, you aren't hearing *His love in the morning.* Are you defensive? If so, you aren't hearing *His love in the morning.* Are you tender, kind, forgiving, humble, generous, patient? Surely, you *are* hearing *His love in the morning*!

173

[18]Do not be drunk with wine, for that is dissipation, but be filled with the Holy Spirit.

Ephesians 5:18

Filled with the Holy Spirit

"What controls you will rule you."

You may not believe a minister is going to confess what you're about to read, but it's all true! In my neighborhood in Texas where I jogged quite regularly, I usually ran by a vacant lot. I couldn't help but scan my eyes over some of the trash thrown in it: beer cans, cigarette packages, plastic Dr. Pepper bottles, Whopper boxes, etc. Sometimes—not always!—I would secretly hope I'd find a brown paper bag filled with $50,000 dollars. You know, the stuff drug dealers throw out the car window while the police are chasing them. (This is not as far fetched as you might think. In a cement culvert five miles from this vacant lot, my secretary's granddaughter found $30,000 cash! I was told that *after* my fantasizing, however.) Then I'd begin to wonder (hallucinating from oxygen debt?) what I would do with all the money. I'd daydream about that until the Spirit of God convicted me: "What are you doing with what you already have?" I would have to slap myself across my mind afresh and ask myself, "Am I a rich son of God or a poor little orphan? Has the Spirit of Christ made me rich or am I a spiritual pauper?"

It is in moments like this that I am acutely aware of what is controlling my heart's desires: the spirit of the flesh versus the Spirit of Christ. Galatians 5:16-17 tells us that a war is raging within us between the Spirit and the flesh. *"But I say, walk by the Spirit, and you will not carry out the desire of the flesh. For the flesh sets its desire against the Spirit, and the Spirit against the flesh; for these are in opposition to one another, so that you may not do the things that you please."* Can you tell whether the Spirit or the flesh is winning the conflict? You need to be able to, in order to live a healthy Christian life.

The Bible commands all believers to *"be filled with the Holy Spirit."* I wonder if this isn't one of the most neglected commands in all the Bible. How many of us deliberately ask Jesus in prayer every day to be filled with His Spirit?

Before we delve into this vital discipline, let me offer a quick reflection on what some Christians call "the Spirit-filled church." The Bible doesn't really talk about Spirit-filled churches, but rather, Spirit-filled individuals. In Acts 2:4, a large group of disciples was *"filled with the Holy Spirit and began to speak with other languages…"* In Acts 4:8, *"Peter, filled with the Holy Spirit, said to the rulers…"* (Other times Peter stands up to preach but the text doesn't mention the Holy Spirit.) Consider also Acts 4:31. *"And when they had prayed, the place where they had gathered together was shaken, and they were all filled with the Holy Spirit, and began to speak the word of God with boldness."* Acts 6:3,5 teaches that deacons are to be sought from among men who are *"full of the Holy Spirit."* A Spirit-filled church must be, then, a body of believers who individually seek to be filled with the Holy Spirit. Do you want that? The health of any church is only as vital as the degree to which its members are seeking to be filled with the Holy Spirit. Who wouldn't want a church like that?

Under His control

Now let's move to an examination of what being filled with the Spirit means, specifically for you. Paul gives us a good answer in Ephesians 5:18. In its context, Paul is working out what it means to love Christ. The first three chapters of the epistle explain how believers are united to Christ by faith. They delineate the indicatives of the gospel—the objective facts: this is what Christ did and since you believe it, this is what's true about you. Once he does that, Paul works out the implications of the believer's union with Christ. What does it look like? He begins Ephesians 5, for example, saying, *"imitate God, as beloved children."* The logic of the gospel is right there. He doesn't say do the right thing and God will accept you; he doesn't say imitate God and as a result He will love you. He says, you *are* beloved children (He made you that!), so act like it. The Christian paradigm for ethics is simply, "Be who you are." Live out the new person God has made you in Christ. So here, Paul gives us a picture of Christ-like living. The presumption is, because we so greatly value Christ's death, love and gift of salvation, surely we'll desire to honor Him by being like Him. Loving Him doesn't save you or change you; He saves you and loves you in order to change you.

Thus, when we get to verse 18, Paul is exhorting us to Christ-like daily conduct, carefully walking before God in wisdom, seeking to understand the will of God. We are to be controlled by principles, not perceptions, by what God reveals, not by how we feel. Then he says, *"And do not get drunk with wine, for that is dissipation, but be filled with the Holy Spirit..."* There are several important points to notice in the grammar:

1. He gives a negative command (*do not get drunk*) followed by a positive command (*be filled*).

2. The picture created is "What controls you?", namely, the contrast between alcohol and the Spirit. That, which fills you, dominates you. It's a graphic image we can all relate to, especially the Ephesian believers. Drunkenness was a major part of the pagan religion of Ephesus; the wine-god Bacchus featured into the worship of Dionysus. Worshippers, once drunk, were supposedly indwelt and controlled by Dionysus, who gave them special powers and abilities. Against that background Paul says, "Every day you wake up, the issue before you is now that you are indwelt by Christ, which will control you, the flesh or the Spirit?"

3. Every Greek verb has several aspects to it; the verb *"be filled"* is conjugated as follows:

Mood: imperative vs. indicative, a command (not an option)

Voice: passive vs. active, meaning the action is happening to you, you are filled *by* the Holy Spirit

Number: plural vs. singular, meaning *everyone* is commanded, not just those who want the Spirit.

Tense: present vs. past: meaning continuous action, so it could be translated *"go on constantly being filled"*

This tells us that we are spiritual dipsomaniacs. A dipsomaniac is always thirsty and always drinking. Therefore, our hearts are like helium balloons—spiritual power leaks out. So we need constant filling. You don't get filled once and go on from there. You need constant filling; that is, coming under the control of the Holy Spirit. I personally assume that any spiritual collateral built up during the day leaks out of me over night!

Put that together and this is the question you must constantly ask yourself: Who or what is controlling me? The issue with filling really isn't how *much* of the Spirit you have. You received all of Him when you were born again. The issue is how much of *you* does the Spirit have? Are you self-consciously giving Him control of your thinking, desires, emotions, perspective, tongue, etc.? The Christian life is a constant yielding, a resisting all that the flesh would want you to do and saying *yes* to the Spirit. Rather than seeing your heart, then, as needing a pouring in of the Spirit, think of filling as a releasing out of the Spirit, a fountain bubbling up to bathe over everything.

Never are we more human than when we are filled with the Spirit. That's why Paul calls drunkenness *"dissipation."* The word refers to a person who extravagantly squanders his means. Just as drunkenness dehumanizes a person, so does the yielding to the flesh. Both states squander the glory of being human. But yielding to the Spirit's control, on the other hand, super-humanizes you. It makes you more like the true man, Jesus Christ. Remember that Jesus was filled with the Spirit at the inauguration of His public ministry. (Matt. 3:16)

You can always expect the Spirit to answer your prayer to be captivated by Him. He's always jealous to do that! It delights Him to control you. However, it grieves Him when you quench Him, when you yield to the flesh. If you need a special endowment for something, perhaps witnessing, speaking, doing something extraordinary for the Lord, ask for special anointing, and expect it.

Before we move to some applications of this wonderful text, it is important that you know, in broad terms, the role of the Spirit in the work of salvation. The *regenerating* Spirit *applies* the work of Christ *for* you; through the gift of faith, the benefits of Christ's death and resurrection are yours. The *sanctifying* Spirit *accomplishes* the work of Christ *in* you; through the means of grace, you are conformed to Christ's image. The *testifying* Spirit *activates* the work of Christ *through* you; by the power of grace, you fulfill Jesus' ministry on earth.

Evidence of the Spirit's control

How do you know you're captivated by the Spirit? There are several ways to answer that question. Some believers have taught that the use of spiritual gifts, especially "sign" gifts like prophecy or tongues, are evidence of the Spirit's filling. While it is true that we can't use gifts without the Spirit—He empowers them—they nevertheless are no guarantee of the Spirit's filling. Paul wrote to the Corinthians, *"you are not lacking in any gift"* (1 Cor. 1:7), yet he chastised them for their lack of spiritual fruit, immaturity, factions and even drunkenness at the Lord's Supper. A better indicator of the Spirit's filling is His fruit, listed in Galatians 5:22-23.

Others teach that inner peace is a mark of the Spirit's fullness. While it is true that peace is a fruit of the Spirit, and that God gives us by the Spirit the peace that passes all understanding, peace isn't always a reliable indicator of the Spirit's control. Our hearts are very capable of creating a peace that isn't of God. I've seen many believers tell me they have His peace, yet they are living in blatant disregard of the Lord's will.

When eager believers strive for doctrinal depth and clarity on lots of biblical issues (a fine thing in itself), the mere presence of such knowledge can deceive people into thinking they are captivated by the Spirit. Again, doctrinal knowledge in itself proves very little. Paul said that we could have all knowledge, yet without love, it is nothing. (1 Cor. 13:1-3)

There are others who point to demonstrative worship, such as raising hands or dancing, as evidence of the Spirit's filling. While the Spirit *may* lead some of us to do that, such displays themselves are difficult to mark definitively as Spirit-led.

How does the text reveal evidence of the Spirit's filling? The command to *be filled,* the main verb in a long sentence encompassing Ephesians 5:18-21, is followed by four participles. Participles modify the main verb in Greek. That means these participles explain what *being filled* looks like. They answer the question, what is the evidence of the Spirit's filling? The four participles are *speaking to one another, singing in your hearts, giving thanks, and submitting.* Each of these is a sermon in itself. It looks like the ambiance the Spirit creates is one of worship, humility, thanksgiving and being other-focused. The opposite of these graces grieve the Holy Spirit, as Paul warns against in Eph. 4:30. *"And do not grieve the Holy Spirit of God, by whom you were sealed for the day of redemption."* Evidently, there are things we do which can either be evidence of the Spirit's presence or His absence. Think about the following contrasts as one way to identify the Spirit's filling.

1. Are you *bold* about the things of God, experiencing a freedom, zeal and fearlessness in speaking the word of God (*"they were filled with the Holy Spirit and began to speak the word of God with boldness"*—Acts 4:31), or are you *bored* with spiritual matters, essentially preoccupied with entertaining your heart with the next toy you discover?

2. Is there a humble *sincerity* marking your life where you honestly seek to repent of sin, or are you stuck in *self-pity* usually wondering, "Why is all this happening to me?"

3.   Are you consciously depending upon the Lord's strength in view of your own *inadequacy*, or is *individualism* producing thoughts like: I can do it! I don't need you! Let me prove something! Are you challenging me?

4.   Do you have an *openness* to the things of God, a searching mentality, a desire to come under the power of God's truth, or are you more *complacent*, perhaps learning just enough to satisfy yourself?

5.   Do you move toward others to *bless* and edify them, or to *use* and manipulate them for your purposes?

6.   Do you *pray*, plan and dream about doing great things for Christ with the spiritual wealth you already have, or do you waste your God-given imagination *dreaming* about things you'll never have or need?

Much more could be said about walking in the power of the Holy Spirit. At a minimum, we need to develop the grace to pray consistently for the Spirit's control over our thoughts and desires, and learn to ask ourselves consistently what is seeking our heart's control, His Spirit or our flesh.

[16]And we have come to know and to believe the love which God has for us. God is love, and the one who abides in love abides in God, and God abides in him. [17]By this, love is perfected with us, that we may have confidence in the day of judgment; because as He is, so also are we in this world. [18]There is no fear in love; but perfect love casts out fear, because fear involves punishment, and the one who fears is not perfected in love. [19]We love, because He first loved us. [20]If someone says, "I love God," and hates his brother, he is a liar; for the one who does not love his brother whom he has seen, cannot love God whom he has not seen. [21]And this commandment we have from Him, that the one who loves God should love his brother also.

1 John 4:16-21

The Power of Perfect Love

"As He is, so also are we in this world. (1 John 4:17)"

After speaking during the Saturday evening session on a retreat for some church leaders and their wives, I joined many in the group as they mingled in the meeting room and played games. At one point, I happened to notice a strange man in the room—he'd apparently slipped into our gathering from the hotel bar adjacent to our meeting room. Evidently, he'd been in the bar for some time! I was startled to see his arms draped over the shoulders of two of the wives in our group—who seemed to be bearing with him in a gracious way. Honestly, my first reaction was, "Don't you go near my wife"; and my second thought was, "I'd like to throw you out of here on your butt."

After a while, I noticed he had left the meeting room, so I figured it was "safe" for me to head up to my room for the night. As I turned down the hall to the elevator, there was the man, talking with two of the men from the church. I caught just a few words of the conversation—they were ministering to him. What conflicting emotions I had! On the one hand, *despair:* How could I be so unloving back there in the room? But on the other, *delight:* I had just witnessed the reality of God's love reaching out to another life, the concrete manifestation of the love of Christ: *the power of perfect love.*

Do you experience that power, both God's love for you and His love moving from you? That's the challenge John sets before you in 1 John 4:16-21: the maturing of Christ's love within. *"If we love one another, God abides in us, and His love is perfected in us."* (v. 12) God is pure love in His essence. He delights to pour out that love into our hearts through Jesus, by the power of the Holy Spirit. *"The love of God has been poured out with in our hearts through the Holy Spirit..."* (Romans 5:5) As His love extends from us to others, it matures, blossoms, comes to fuller expression and reaches its highest pinnacle. There is good news for this love-starved world. *"God is love, and the one who abides in love abides in God, and God abides in him."* (1 John 4:16)

God has a love-renewal program for this strife-filled world; it's called Christianity. God's goal for the earth is not just to forgive sinners, but also to fill the world with people who have been transformed by the love of Jesus Christ. God *alone* has what this world needs, and He pours it out through His Son that it might displace our self-concern and naturally splash out on others.

How do you know you experience the power of God's perfect love? John says we know it by its casting out power, by its displacing power. We'll examine in this chapter the two dehumanizing realities it casts out: perfect love casts out *fear*; perfect love casts out *hate*.

Perfect love casts out fear.

Most people give intellectual assent to God's love...just as people acknowledge that flying is the safest way to travel. But, haven't you had a conversation like this?

Do you know that flying is the safest way to travel?
Yes.

So how often do you fly?
Never! I'm afraid the plane will crash.

Notice how John exposes the heart of trusting God's love: fear vs. confidence, *"there is no fear in love."* (v. 18) When God pours His love into us—1 John 4:13 says the Holy Spirit convinces us of the love of God, proven in the sending of His Son—what can we be certain it contains? Do you look at the side of your cereal box to see what percentage of daily requirements you're getting? The box of God's love contains vast portions, yes, 100% of the daily requirement of mercy, grace, kindness, patience, pity, strength, and joy; and it also contains not an ounce of fear (terror). There is no terror in God's love.

But there's more. *"Perfect love casts out fear."* There is power in the love of God to displace from our hearts the natural fear which lies within us—not self-preserving fear which keeps you from driving at insane speeds, not fear of the Lord (reverence, awe, amazement at God's glory), but fear of His wrath. We all know deep in the inner man that we are not what God made us to be, that we don't give God what we know He requires: total allegiance, obedience and worship. Fear of God's judgment on our heart's natural condition lies latent in the psyche of man; therefore, we avoid Him, stay away from Him and try to put Him out of our minds. Why else do you think people naturally think so little about God, and naturally create a god who has no wrath toward sin?

We attempt to do much to suppress fear of God's wrath: strive for success, stay busy at church, ignore it, maybe we even "get religious." Some people hide behind their religion, thinking it makes them a good person. But most religion is ultimately riddled with fear, because it can never get rid of punishment. Verse 18 says, *"fear involves punishment."* The only time I feared my parents was when I blew it and knew I deserved to be punished. Funny thing how there isn't much enjoyment in punishment! Fear cripples and paralyzes.

What does it take to displace our fear of God's punishment? *"Perfect love casts out fear."* Where do you find that? You may have been searching your whole life to be perfectly loved, but God says He is the only one who can do it. His love *only* is powerful to banish all fears of punishment on the judgment day. Perfect love is what we receive in the Lord Jesus Christ. In the gospel, Jesus declares, "I'll take you just as you are, *but* I'll make you far more holy and morally beautiful than you ever dreamt possible."

God loves us in His Son, for His Son's sake, and on the basis of—because of, predicated upon—His Son's flawlessly righteous life. In other words, the reason God loves you isn't in you. The love of God for sinners—those who fail to give Him what He rightly deserves—does not exist apart from Jesus. In fact, the text takes it even farther; you can never experience the love of God in Jesus Christ *unless* Jesus is raised from the dead *"...that we may have confidence for the day of judgment, because as He is, so also are we in this world."* (v. 17)

What a staggering claim! Whatever Jesus is right now, so are we who have been united to Him by faith. Here is the wonderful doctrine of union with Christ. Your faith in Jesus unites you to Him such that, what is true of Him, is forever true of you too—true of you *now*, in this world, not *simply* in the next.

This is the Christianity that promises too much! Some people think Christianity is like all other religions, a code of ethics based on the teaching of a famous, winsome man. No way! The Christianity of the Bible is far better than that. Do you see that there's still fear in that? How do you know you've done enough? What hope is there for people who know they can't muster up the moral perfection God requires for His holy presence? Religion generates fear; Christ dispels it! How? By His unfailing grace, Jesus shares with us freely the spoils of His life, death and resurrection. Jesus says to you, "When you put your trust in *Me*, in what I've done and only in *Me*, when you believe and rest upon *My* obedience and death, you have what is mine."

Notice how critical the resurrection is in this equation. The verse says *as He is...* not as He was or will be. Jesus is *now* the Lord of glory and King of Kings, never to change. But before the cross, He couldn't save you from your sins; it took His death on the cross to pay satisfaction for your sins. Plus, if Jesus merely died, at best as an example of supreme sacrificial love, you still have no savior. Only by the resurrection do we have the Father's guarantee that His Son's life and death are acceptable. In the resurrection, the Father pronounces complete satisfaction with the work of His Son.

The proof is Jesus, ascending to the right hand of God, having sat down. That means He has finished His work of redeeming His own, having once and for all purchased them with His own blood (life and death).

Are you living as if you need to make yourself more "purchase-able" to the Father? If you are, it is because you don't believe the promise of the gospel. *"As he is, so also are we in this world"*— right now!

The Father asks no more legal righteousness of Jesus; neither does He ask any more of those united to Him. The Father smiles upon His Son in utter delight. "My beloved, enjoy My presence forever, bask in My affection." As beautiful as Jesus looks to the Father, so do you. Jesus will never die for sins again; the agony is over; neither will you die to pay for your sins. (However, we will all die physically because of sin.) Jesus is alive in the Spirit forever. So are you now, though we experience only a part of what we will be. Jesus is through with the realm of sin, so you no longer have to sin. (See Romans 6:6.) What does Jesus fear right now? Nothing! Neither should you! Remember, *fear involves judgment*, but Jesus faced the judgment of God on the cross. His wrath is spent, emptied, never to be seen again by His own. Hence, John declares, *"He loved us and sent His Son to be the propitiation for our sins."* (1 John 4:10) *"Propitiation"* means Jesus removed our sins and God's wrath for those sins.

So, suppose you really blow it. You continue to struggle with besetting sins, and thus fear creeps into your heart. As you confess your sins, go look in the cup of God's wrath, that vessel of wine foaming with His vengeance. (Jer. 25:15) What's in it? Not a drop. Jesus drank it all for you, in love. *Perfect love casts out fear.* To the extent we fear, God's love doesn't control us. If you're afraid of God's punishment, you're saying He failed in His Son. If you fear judgment from the Father, how can you serve Him freely and joyfully?

187

As he is, so also are we in this world. (1 John 4:17) What are you in this world? You are the delight of the Father. If God had a refrigerator in heaven, your picture would be on it! The Father says to Jesus, I don't require any more from you. When God in the gospel says to you, "I don't require any more from you," if your heart knows that love you will say, "Good, I'll give you all I have. I'll gladly live boldly and fearlessly for you!" The love of God, which casts out fear, replaces it with confidence, bold living before a God who completely accepts us. You know that confidence by praying as Paul does in 2 Thessalonians 2:16-17. *"Now may our Lord Jesus Christ Himself and God our Father, who has loved us and given us eternal comfort and good hope by grace, comfort and strengthen your hearts in every good work and word."*

Perfect love casts out hate.

If perfect love casts out fear, and confidence replaces fear, then perfect love is also powerful to cast out hate; God's love displaces hatred.

If in practice, you hate your fellow believer, that is, if you want him dead, want to have nothing to do with him, you wish him ill, you can ignore his suffering under his afflictions, you don't want God to love him, then you obviously don't love God or abide in His love. Your claim to know God is a lie. In fact, if your perspective is, I don't buy all this love stuff—all that matters is I love God and my family—then you've created a false God. There is no God that isn't pure love, and He desires His love to be expressed through you. 1 John 4:21 is a single command: *"And this commandment we have from Him, that the one who loves God should love his brother also."* If you can so readily dismiss yourself from the love demand, you don't understand that God could have justly said to you, "I hate you; I want you forever out of My presence."

How can you have the love of Jesus and hate someone who Jesus loves? Hatred is usually borne of pride. "I don't like how you compare to *me*, what you do to *me*, what you don't do for *me*."

Hatred is about self-need, taking. Love is about giving, service. Therefore, love always initiates. *"We love, because He first loved us."* (v. 19) Pride waits to be loved; love waits for nothing. How do you love? Ask and act. Search and serve.

Ask the right question. Often we ask ourselves how we feel about that person, or are we getting from them what we think we deserve. Wrong questions! Love asks, "What is best for this person?" You can always serve another's best interests, regardless of feelings. "What does this one need? What can I do or say or give to build them up?" Sometimes that's affirmation, sometimes maybe a word of correction. The goal is always to beautify, to make them more in character like Jesus is in His resurrected glory. Ask the question, "What can I do to increase this person's confidence before God, to alleviate his or her fears?" Notice how Paul defines love in 1 Thessalonians 5:14-15. *"And we urge you, brethren, admonish the unruly, encourage the fainthearted, help the weak, be patient with all men. See that no one repays another with evil for evil, but always seek after that which is good for one another and for all men."*

Obviously, it isn't very helpful merely to ask the right question without acting accordingly. The Bible sees through our motives in this regard. James 2:15-16 warns, *"If a brother or sister is without clothing and in need of daily food, and one of you says to them, 'Go in peace, be warmed and be filled,' and yet does not give them what is necessary for their body, what use is that?"* As we act practically to meet the needs of our neighbor, we can be certain that Jesus will supply all the grace necessary, in super-abundant quantity, for His own glory.

[11]A man's discretion makes him slow to anger, And it is his glory to overlook a transgression.

Proverbs 19:11

The Forgiving Heart

"You are most beautiful when you are most forgiving."

Are you tired of the beauty rat race? Are you worn out trying to look pretty, smart, physically fit, bubbly, successful? Relax…there's a way to win the race. Take the advice I'm going to give you, and you will shine, you'll be more beautiful than you ever imagined, more personally glorious in character. How can you be sure? God promises!

Proverbs 19:11 says your boast, your greatness, your beauty, your glory is to *"overlook a transgression."* The word *"overlook"* conveys the idea of passing by or moving beyond. It doesn't mean ignore, that's impossible. God never asks you to pretend sin isn't real. The idea is, when you are sinned against, keep going, keep that relationship moving, *"so far as it depends upon you."* (Rom. 12:18) In other words, don't let anger stall you. Don't let unforgiveness put you in a rut. Don't let a root of bitterness tie you to the ground. Don't hold a grudge in your hands, so that they're not open to receive God's other blessings.

Consider four truths Proverbs 19:11 assumes.

You will have sins committed against you. This verse is given to people who live in a fallen world where there is a lot of sin. There are no sinless people on this earth. You have been and will be sinned against by all kinds of people (believers and unbelievers), even those you think shouldn't! (Why do you expect *anyone* to be perfect in a fallen world?)

You will respond in one way or another. We don't have to pretend sins don't hurt! The natural temptation is to be angry and unforgiving, to fail to get past it. Notice how the first half of the verse, *"wisdom makes you slow to anger,"* sets up the last half, *"it is your glory to overlook a transgression."* How you respond determines whether you live in a self-made prison of resentment, or move forward in freedom.

You don't have to get stuck in bitter resentment. That's why the verse holds out the promise for you of a distinct spiritual beauty. Hebrews 12:14-15 warns about a root of bitterness.

God is sovereign over these hurts. Implicit behind this verse is the biblical assertion that God is in control. Prov. 16:9 says, *"The mind of man plans his way, but the Lord directs his steps."* Prov. 19:21 *"Many are the plans in a man's heart, but the counsel of the Lord, it will stand."* Therefore, you can be confident your conflicts are ordained by God *for your good* (Rom. 8:28).

Everything God is doing in your life is designed to make you like Christ, especially afflictions and difficulties in relationships. God uses these to help you grow, to help you see your sin (faults of others are often like mirrors reflecting what we hide from ourselves), to help you see how much grace you need. Hurts help you see how great is His mercy and comfort to you, they help you experience God's redemptive power and help you love others in ways they might never have known.

If God has His *purposes* in the offenses we suffer, then He also must have the *proscription* to remedy the injury. That means we have to use God's remedy, not our homespun concoctions. You will be tempted to treat the pain only, not the injury. Perhaps you'll want to retreat, throw up walls of self-protection and not let anyone in to your heart. Perhaps you'll promise yourself never to take risks in relationships. These are decidedly not God's solutions. The Triune God is utterly committed to harmony. What is God's remedy? How do you overlook, pass by or go beyond another's transgressions?

Proverbs 19:11 doesn't say. It leaves us longing for more. Therefore, this verse catapults us to the New Testament. There we see the great transgression eliminator: the cross of Jesus. At the cross, Jesus promises to remove your sins from you! There is only *one way* to move past others' offenses: put the cross between you and them. *"Forgive one another, as Christ has forgiven you..."* (Col. 3:13)

There is an amazing power in the cross, experienced by those who take the time to stand beneath it. When you ask for an open, humble heart, to know God, to see His glory, you will see in the cross both the horrible consequences of your sin (putting Jesus there, holding your transgressions) and the unspeakable wonder of His love for you (willingly staying there). The cross is the supreme concrete demonstration of the love of God. *"God demonstrates his own love for us in that while we were yet sinners, Christ died for us..."* (Rom. 5:8)

The glorious revelation of the cross is divine love for sinners. That's why Jesus said in John 15:12, *"love one another, just as I have loved you."* You would never know the love of Christ if He hadn't overlooked your transgressions, and taken you with Him to glory. That's the basis for the promise: *"love truly covers all transgressions."* (Prov. 10:12) 1 Peter 4:8 echoes this. *"Keep fervent in your love for one another, because love covers a multitude of sins."* Love covers transgressions means you refuse to harp on them, to reveal or expose them; instead, you bury any reason to put yourself above others.

God's word teaches that the issue when others hurt you is, "Can you still love them?" In a sense, you don't know how much you love until you have to love the unlovely. God's agape love is unconditional; it doesn't set conditions or terms, such as, I'll love you when you're nice to me. *"Love does not take into account a wrong suffered."* (1 Cor. 13:5)

Jesus explains that a startling thing will happen if you stay long at the cross. Your vision will be improved! *"Take the log out of your eye, then you'll actually be able to see the speck in another's."* But what if another person objectively has sinned significantly against you? It is cause for at least two responses from you.

First, it is a cause for pity and patience. Can't you thank God for the grace you've received not to have been given over to sin as much as the one who sinned against you? Realistically, what person among us could claim to have sinned less, except by the sheer restraining mercy of God? Verses such as 2 Timothy 2:23-25, remind us that God does the changing. *"And the Lord's bondservant must not be quarrelsome, but kind to all, able to teach, patient when wronged, with gentleness correcting those who are in opposition, if perhaps God may grant them repentance leading to the knowledge of the truth, and they may come to their senses and escape the snare of the devil, having been held captive by him to do his will."*

Second, it is a cause for self-examination. What's going on in your heart? Why *would* you stop and not pass by? Often it boils down to, "How dare you offend me!" But why not offend you? Who made you a person exempt from being offended? What do you believe about yourself ... to assert the right not to overlook an offense? Is your unwillingness to overlook a transgression really a covert attempt to bolster your own righteousness; that is, to be God, who alone has the right not to forgive? If you are unwilling to try to bring the other person along with you, are you saying that they really aren't worth it? Can you tell Jesus they aren't worth it? Why can't you take an offender with you to the throne of grace, where we *all* find help in time of need?

Now you may protest, "Well I *have* overlooked, I just don't care to deal with that person!" But does God treat you that way in the gospel? Or is it much better than that? God proclaims in the gospel of Christ, "I forgive you, and now I adopt you! Now that I've forgiven you, I've only just begun to open the floodgates of My blessings! Now that I've bought you as My own, by the blood of My Son, come share in all the riches that are His!" (Rom. 8:32)

194

Archibald Alexander, a Presbyterian theologian who served ten years as president of Hampden-Sydney College, said, "Increasing solicitude for the salvation of men, sorrow on account of their sinful and miserable condition, and a disposition tenderly to warn sinners of their danger, evince a growing state of piety. It is also a strong evidence of growth in grace when you can bear injuries and provocations with meekness and when you can from the heart desire the temporal and eternal welfare of your bitterest enemies."

Here's the test to see if you're truly overlooking offenses. Will you give that person the benefit of the doubt—attributing to them the best of motives? Will you concretely promote their best—including your serving them? Will you pray for them, as you would want God to bless you? Can you see them as someone sinned against and warped by the fall, desperately needing your pity and compassion? Will you pay the price for their sin (all sin involves a debt) with the riches lavished upon you in Christ? That's your greatest glory, because when you overlook another's offense, never are you more like Christ!

Because of the gospel, we can come freely to Christ with our frail, resentful hearts. We can tell Jesus we want, sadly, to punish the other person for what they did to us. We can hear Jesus say, "It's alright. I'll take care of you. Let me do the punishing in My time and in My way. I'll give you enough grace to absorb the cost of what's been inflicted upon you. Just as I will not hold against you what you inflicted on Me, don't you hold it against them." Therein is a tremendous freedom to end the rat race of proving your self worth and to adorn the glorious heart of Christ.

[1]Remind them to be subject to rulers, to authorities, to be obedient, to be ready for every good deed, [2]to malign no one, to be uncontentious, gentle, showing every consideration for all men. [3]For we also once were foolish ourselves, disobedient, deceived, enslaved to various lusts and pleasures, spending our life in malice and envy, hateful, hating one another. [4]But when the kindness of God our Savior and His love for mankind appeared, [5]He saved us, not on the basis of deeds which we have done in righteousness, but according to His mercy, by the washing of regeneration and renewing by the Holy Spirit, [6]whom He poured out upon us richly through Jesus Christ our Savior, [7]that being justified by His grace we might be made heirs according to the hope of eternal life.

Titus 3:1-8

The Communicating Heart

*"Your communication style will either condemn or commend
the very message of grace you seek to convey."*

I don't know why they did it, but when I was in grade
school, my parents gave my brothers and me boxing gloves
for Christmas. We used the oval braided rug in the family
room as our boxing ring. I'll never forget one time sparring
with my older brother Dave; we were interrupted when
Mom called from the kitchen. He stopped, dropped his
hands at his side, and looked away from me toward the
kitchen...I couldn't resist! All the years of being picked on,
pounded upon, being last because I was the youngest...I
threw my strongest upper cut to his jaw and knocked him
out cold! It felt so good...but there has to be a better way to
communicate pent-up frustration.

I'm happy to tell you that since that episode I have not
physically hit another human being. I'm ashamed to admit,
however, that it's not because I've outgrown such a
childish way to handle frustration. I still carry in my heart a
tendency to take a jab—not with fists—but with destructive
swords of attitude and word. The text we just read assumes
we all have this proclivity to defend or attack. How can we
change? Is there hope for sheathing this sword we tend to
wield so quickly? Paul says *yes*.

First, he *proscribes* a better way to live. Titus 3:2 says
there's a better way to communicate with others than with

swords that aim to hurt. Paul frames for us a four-sided ring in which Godly communication can occur.

Malign no one. The word means to slander or to treat with contempt. In the context of Titus 3, Paul has the pagan government authorities in view. Believers were not to treat them with contempt, though they probably had multiple reasons to do so. I'm certain we all have our list of exceptions registered with God in heaven, but Paul says *"no one."* Not even someone with whom you have vehement differences. It certainly follows that by all means we slander no one within the household of faith.

Be uncontentious. If you want to fight with others, you've stepped outside the ring of godly communication. Paul says the ring isn't for fighting, but rather patient instruction. *"The Lord's bondservant must not quarrel, but instead be kind to everyone, able to teach, not resentful; those who oppose he must gently instruct..."* (2 Tim. 2:24) Doesn't the book of Proverbs indicate that it's not so much fun living with a contentious woman? (Prov. 21:9) How much less edifying is your arguing about theology with someone who wants to fight? That's what Paul proscribes: don't fight with people; we have sufficient warfare with the devil. When your pursuit of the truth crosses a boundary outside the ring, the Bible says, "there's a better way."

Be gentle. Gentleness is a fruit of the Spirit and a qualification for elder, the word Jesus uses to describe Himself in Matt. 11:29. *"I am gentle and humble in heart."* This self-revelation is in the context of Christ calling sinners to come to Him. He will give rest to weary and burdened souls. This is Paul's better way: a quality of communication reflecting Jesus' gentleness, a welcoming word assuring rest and refreshment. By His grace, it can happen: a discussion with a person of another persuasion, restrained by gentleness.

Show every consideration for all men. Here is the fourth side of Paul's four-sided ring of godly communication. The contest, for Paul, isn't winning the argument. We may have won a thousand arguments with unbelievers, our spouses, our children and Christian friends, but we may have lost the person. If you have all knowledge without love, you have nothing. (1 Cor. 13:1-2) The contest is, of course, contending for the faith, but doing it in such a way that your words and attitudes express forbearance and patience, leaving the other person thinking, "I may not agree with you right now but I sure appreciate the courteous way you present what you passionately believe."

Ponder these qualities for a moment. Doesn't it pierce you to be on the receiving end of their opposites? Don't you want your daughter treated by her husband the way Paul proscribes? Do you want your son's baseball coach to pound him with the opposite of these, to be maligning, contentious, having no consideration for his weaknesses as a person? Do you want your doctor to embody these graces as he tends to you in your pain? Then by all means let us crown our heads with these jewels as we communicate within the household of faith.

Second, Paul under girds his *proscription* with a *principle*. The first six words of Titus 3:3, *"for we also once ourselves were"* form a simple principle for Paul's better way to communicate: I understand, because I stand under! Paul sets forth this principle because he knows how difficult it is for sinners to find consistently the better way. I read verse 2 and think, how can I be like that when someone attacks me, when I have to defend the truth, when the heart of the gospel is on the line? Paul's answer is, just don't forget what you once were. This isn't simply a proof text for total depravity; it's the sheath that restrains the sword I so quickly want to draw against folks who cross me. Verse 2 *assumes* there are plenty of folks you just don't like, who are sitting ducks for your righteous criticism. It *is* a fallen world. Paul is saying, "Always relate to others *consciously understanding* what you once were." Rather than assuming a posture of "I stand over you to critique you," verse 3 says, "I understand because I stand under!"

I understand that you may be *foolish, or disobedient, or deceived, or enslaved to some sins, or hateful*...because I had the same junk in my heart. And it didn't go away when I was converted; it's just that now in Christ I'm fighting it daily by the grace of the Holy Spirit. I understand what sin does to people, because I *stand under the cross.* The cross exposed me; it revealed my sin; it showed *me* to be hateful, deceived, disobedient to God. The cross stripped me of my self-justifying goodness. Standing under the cross, I saw the love of Christ for me.

So now, when I have difficulty with you, or your theology or your perspectives, I have to understand first, *"I am what I am by the grace of God."* (1 Cor. 15:10) Considering all the grace I've received, I should be much better than I am. Grace has shown me that my weaknesses are too strong for me, that I can't conquer these temptations with my own resources. Without the restraining power of Christ, I'm going to slip into everything Titus 3:3 delineates. Verse 3, therefore, drives me to Jesus; Jesus then disarms me. "How can you punch your brother with the same hands that bloodied me on the cross? Hasn't my love for you, my mercy, forgiveness and patience, driven you to drop your sword?"

Next, Paul describes God's *provision* for a better way to live. Lest we miss the obvious, Paul spells out in Titus 3:4-6 the content of God's grace to us through the work of the Triune God: the Father lovingly sending the Son; the Son saving us by His righteousness and death; and the Spirit regenerating and renewing our hearts. Paul placards the gospel as the only motivator to stay in the four-sided ring of godly communication.

How do you know the gospel is driving your attitude toward others? You see yourself as a debtor and the others as potential heirs of eternal life. Even more, it boils down to how you fundamentally see Jesus. Is He primarily a lawgiver? Someone who makes demands, who basically says, "Keep trying harder, I'll bless you when you get it together"? If so, either you will be frustrated with yourself and consequently demanding of others, lashing out at them; or you will be pridefully judgmental, intolerant and condescending.

But if Jesus is, for you, primarily a Savior, one who kept the law in your place, who freed you from all condemnation, who delights to lavish upon you goodness upon goodness, then your demeanor will principally be peaceful and gracious. You won't have the need to prove yourself because you are an heir of eternal life. Winning the person for Christ's sake is more important than winning the argument.

Finally, we embrace the *product* of God's provision. The gospel produces grace-filled communication. Paul captures this so eloquently in Eph. 4:29. *"Let no unwholesome word proceed from your mouth, but only such a word as is good for edification according to the need of the moment, that it may give* grace *to those who hear."* *"Let your speech always be with* grace, *seasoned as it were with salt, so that you may know how to respond to each person."* (Col. 4:6)

Paul sees the tongue as a three-legged stool, which works only when all three legs are soundly in place.

The leg of holiness: (Titus 2:14) *"He gave himself for us, that He might redeem us from every lawless deed and purify for himself a people for His own possession, zealous for good deeds."* You are set apart for God's personal use; your tongue is a stool leg chiseled by His hand.

The leg of wholeness: "speaking the truth in love..." (Eph. 4:15) Your communication is to be whole, cut from the eternal word of God. Truth without love is harsh; love without truth is impotent.

The leg of humility: "Let each one think more highly of the other than himself..." (Phil. 2:4) The gospel rightly applied will produce communication that seeks the best for the other person. In other words, the *demeanor* of our speech should reveal what we've received, *grace*, and the *content* of our speech should reveal what we offer, *truth!*

That is the quality of communication the gospel produces. You need to be as concerned with your *demeanor* as you are with your *doctrine*, with your *motive* as you are with your *message*, lest the way you speak deny the message you hope to convey. Why is Paul concerned with *how* we communicate? Because every time we communicate, it is another opportunity to reveal the beauty of Christ: that He has come not to *hit* sinners, but to *heal* them.

How we speak to others reveals the overflow of the heart, it exposes which Spirit possesses us. Christ is exceedingly jealous to reveal His beauty, wonder, love, wisdom and grace through the Spirit He has poured out into our hearts. What a sacred trust and privilege we've been given!

Let us be accused of loving sinners too much! Let the world charge us with extravagant love and forbearance with one another.

I'll close with a story about Patsy. I met her through my daughter's softball team. We talked in some depth at one of the picnics after the season ended. The conversation moved to the Lord. She basically is a theological liberal, who once accepted but then self-consciously rejected conservative, biblical Christianity. We ended our first discussion very open-ended. I saw her on regular occasions at a bagel shop where I meet with students. Then one time we had the opportunity to pick up where we left off. Rather than try to prove her theology wrong, I sought to understand her point of view. She explained her liberal views and the reasons she had moved toward them. The conservatives she hung out with years ago, she said, were self-righteous, smug and critical, a glaring contradiction in attitude to what they said they believed. So she left the Bible. In the midst of our discussion, I realized two things. One, I was so well trained in theology and apologetics that I could have demonstrated numerous inconsistencies in her perspective. But, the Lord also convicted me that the way in which I sought to dialogue with her would either condemn or commend the very gospel of grace I wanted her to embrace.

We had a good talk; I did challenge some of her positions. We ended peacefully. Two weeks later, I saw her at a softball game. First thing out of her mouth was, "Mike, when are we going to continue our discussion?" That is the kind of response we pray that grace-filled communication will foster, to the glory of the One who constantly fills us with His grace.

[23]Watch over your heart with all diligence, for from it flow the springs of life.

Proverbs 4:23

A Brief Conclusion

"Grace which, like the Lord, the giver, never fails from age to age."[*]

We began with a question: Are you as impressed with God as you should be? We've tried to demonstrate that an honest answer is *no, because our hearts are a mess.* Sin does a number on all of us by deceiving and creating false gods, which ultimately destroy us. The heart is, said John Calvin, "a veritable factory of idols." Only in the gospel of the Lord Jesus Christ is there hope for forgiveness and change. And hope we should! *"I am confident that He who began a good work in you will bring it to completion at the day of Christ Jesus."* (Phil. 1:6) *"Now the God of hope fill you with all joy and peace in believing, that you may abound in hope by the power of the Holy Spirit."* (Romans 15:13)

We desperately need Christ, all that He promises, all of the time, working in all of the heart. When we cast ourselves helplessly upon the Lord, rest assured He finds that irresistible! He can't help but come to our aide. *"And may the Lord direct your hearts into the love of God and steadfastness of Christ."* (2 Thes. 3:5)

Only the humble heart will make such a cry. Ask Him to humble you, and He will. But don't stop there. Ask God to lavish upon you all of the riches of Christ. The Puritans would say, for every look you take at your sin, take ten looks at Jesus! Jesus will reveal Himself as Conqueror of both the guilt and power of sin. If

---

[*] John Newton, "Glorious Things of Thee Are Spoken"

He died for you, He'll withhold nothing from you. *"He who did not spare His own Son, but delivered Him up for us all, how will he not also with Him freely give us all things?"* (Romans 8:32)

While we really have no confidence in ourselves, we ought to trust wholeheartedly in the sufficiency of grace. *"But we should always give thanks to God for you, brethren beloved by the Lord, because God has chosen you from the beginning for salvation through sanctification by the Spirit and faith in the truth. And it was for this He called you through our gospel, that you may gain the glory of our Lord Jesus Christ."* (2 Thes. 2:13-14) My pastor during my seminary years, Jack Miller, used to say, "Cheer up, you are a lot worse than you know." He was right. Grace frees us to have joy in spite of our struggles with sin. Grace takes our focus off of ourselves and puts it upon the One who is the unending fountain of God's refreshing mercy.

SCRIPTURE INDEX

Scripture Index

Proverbs (cont.)

5:1-14	48
5:3-4	48
5:3-6	42
5:6	46
5:11-14	45
5:15-23	48
5:21	43
5:22	47
5:23	45
6:2	48
6:23	46
7	48
7:2-3	66
7:3	67
7:25	46
8:11	44
9:1-6	41
9:6	44
9:10	44
9:13f	22
9:13-16	41
10:12	193
10:17	45
10:22	146, 149
11:20	43
11:21	42
12:15	19, 60
12:22	43
12:27	16
12:28	45
13:1	46
13:20	47
14:2	21, 75
14:12	19, 43, 60, 66, 76, 142

Proverbs (cont.)

16:2	43, 60
16:3	49
16:4	49, 77
16:9	49, 192
16:17	46
16:25	43
18:11	148
19:3	21, 141
19:4	75
19:11	190, 191, 193
19:19	48
19:21	49, 192
20:9	23, 170
20:24	49
21:2	19, 43, 142
21:9	198
21:16	42, 48
21:21	42
21:31	49
22:15	19
22:24-25	47
25:16	47
25:26	16
25:28	48
28:13-14	48, 54
28:26	38, 44
29:8-9	47
29:25	47
30:7-9	148
30:12	43, 60, 140
30:16	53
Ecclesiastes 3:11	29

1 Timothy 6:7-10	148	James (cont.)	
		2:15-16	189
2 Timothy	137	2:16	15
2:23-25	194	3:9	28
2:24	198	4:4	55, 157
3:16	68		
4	138	1 Peter	
4:9-10	137	1:3	77
		1:8-9	10
Titus		1:16	63
2:14	68, 201	2:8	77
3	198	2:11	118
3:1-8	196	2:24	91
3:2	197, 199	4:8	193
3:3	199, 200	5:6	62
3:4-6	200		
		2 Peter	
Philemon 24	137	1:3	68
		1:4	122
Hebrews		1:12,13	23
1:3	120	2:19	18, 47, 53
3	168	3:1	23
3:12-13	139	3:14	125
4:12	61	3:18	10
7:25	121		
9:27	78	1 John	
10	168	1:9	23
10:14, 19-22	169	2:1-2	145
10:24-25	145	3:2	126
12:14-15	192	3:8	93
		4:10	187
James		4:12	184
1:14-15	53	4:13	184
1:14-17	146	4:16	184
1:18	77	4:16-21	182, 183
1:21	69	4:17	183, 186, 188

About the Author

Mike Sharrett graduated from Gettysburg College (B.A. Philosophy) in 1978 and received an M.Ed. from the University of Virginia (Counselor Education) in 1979. He joined the University of Virginia faculty as an assistant director in the Office of Career Planning and Placement, counseling students and teaching an undergraduate course in career planning. Sensing a call to the ministry in 1982, he joined the staff of Trinity PCA in Charlottesville as an assistant pastor. In 1985, Mike attended Westminster Theological Seminary in Philadelphia (M.Div.) and returned to Trinity as an associate pastor, being ordained in 1988.

In 1992, Mike was called to church plant in Ft. Worth, TX. During those 12 years, he was elected to the board of trustees of Westminster Seminary Philadelphia and taught several practical theology classes at the Westminster Dallas campus. He also served on the state committee for Reformed University Fellowship, and was delighted to see a strong RUF develop at Texas Christian University in Ft. Worth.

Desiring to church plant again, Mike moved to Lynchburg, VA in 2004 to lead a regional church planting movement. His wife of 27 years, Janice, is a teacher in a Christian classical school. They have three children, Mike, Luke and Laura. Mike enjoys most sports, especially golf and bodysurfing.

Printed in the United States
53785LVS00003B/103-120

9 780974 233130